THE MEXICANS
HOW THEY LIVE AND WORK

HOW THEY LIVE AND WORK

Volumes in the series:

THE ARGENTINES, by Dereck H. N. Foster
THE AUSTRALIANS, by Nancy Learmonth
THE CHINESE, by T. R. Tregear
THE DUTCH, by Ann Hoffmann
THE EGYPTIANS, by Shirley Kay
THE FINNS AND THE LAPPS, by John L. Irwin
THE FRENCH, by Joseph T. Carroll
THE GREEKS, by T. R. B. Dicks
THE IRISH, by Martin Wallace
THE ITALIANS, by Andrew Bryant
THE JAPANESE, by W. Scott Morton
THE NORWEGIANS, by Arthur Spencer
THE RUSSIANS, by W. H. Parker
THE SPANIARDS, by Michael Perceval
THE SWEDES, by Paul Britten Austin
THE WEST GERMANS, by Reginald Peck
THE WEST INDIANS, by Basil E. Cracknell

The Mexicans

HOW THEY LIVE AND WORK

Peter Calvert

PRAEGER PUBLISHERS
New York

Published in the United States of America in 1975
by Praeger Publishers, Inc.
111 Fourth Avenue, New York, N.Y. 10003

© Peter Calvert, 1975

All rights reserved

Library of Congress Cataloging in Publication Data

Calvert, Peter.
 The Mexicans: how they live and work.

 SUMMARY: A basic survey of Mexico and its people.
 1. Mexico—Juvenile literature. [1. Mexico]
I. Title.
F1208.5.C28   917.2'03'82   74-17467

ISBN 0-275-26010-0

Printed in Great Britain

Contents

1 **THE COUNTRY AND THE PEOPLE**   11
The concept of Mexico · physical characteristics · climate · vegetation · the people · chief historical landmarks · the population · religion · the language · national characteristics

2 **THE CAPITAL AND THE REGIONS**   38
The capital · the Core · the West and South Pacific states · Yucatán · the north · Baja California · the Gulf region · Mexicans abroad

3 **HOW THE COUNTRY IS RUN**   54
The Constitution · the president · the ruling party · other political parties · the electoral system · the legal system · the states · the municipalities · the civil service · currency and taxation · the economy · the armed forces · the police · national symbols

4 **HOW THEY LIVE**   82
Housing · food and drink · private consumption · health · social security

5 **HOW THEY WORK**   99
Agriculture · stockraising · forestry · fishing · sisal · iron and steel · gold and silver · other minerals · petroleum · electric power · cement · textiles · tourism · commerce

6 **HOW THEY GET ABOUT**   119
Railways · roads · air · ports · traffic · mail and telephone

7 **HOW THEY LEARN**   132
Primary education · secondary education · technical · university · further education

Contents

8 **HOW THEY AMUSE THEMSELVES** 142
Fiestas · bullfighting · other sports · the cinema · radio and television · music · the visual arts · literature and the Press

9 **HINTS FOR VISITORS** 156
Clothing · travel documents · how to get there · hotels · food and health · language · tourist information · souvenirs

INDEX 164

List of Illustrations

'El Castillo', Chichén Itzá (*Diana Farrow*)	33
Paseo de la Reforma, Mexico City (*Mexican National Tourist Council*)	33
Ploughing with mules near Mazatlán, Sinaloa (*D. J. Fox*)	34
Pioneer farmer building his own house, State of Chiapas (*D. J. Fox*)	34
City market at Mérida, Yucatán (*Diana Farrow*)	51
Country market at Zaachila, near Oaxaca (*D. J. Fox*)	51
'Butterfly fishermen' of Lake Patzcuaro (*D. J. Fox*)	52
Sisal fibre drying in the sun, State of Tamualipas (*D. J. Fox*)	52
Oil refinery at Poza Rica, Veracruz (*Mexican National Tourist Council*)	85
Taking drinking water to Mexico City (*D. J. Fox*)	85
Family walk in the Alameda, Mexico City (*D. J. Fox*)	86
Village procession, State of Oaxaca (*D. J. Fox*)	86
Public letter writers, Mexico City (*D. J. Fox*)	103
Palace of Sport, Mexico City (*Mexican National Tourist Council*)	103
Presidential parade, Mexico City (*D. J. Fox*)	104

Maps

States, towns and land communications	8–9
Relief	15
National air routes	125

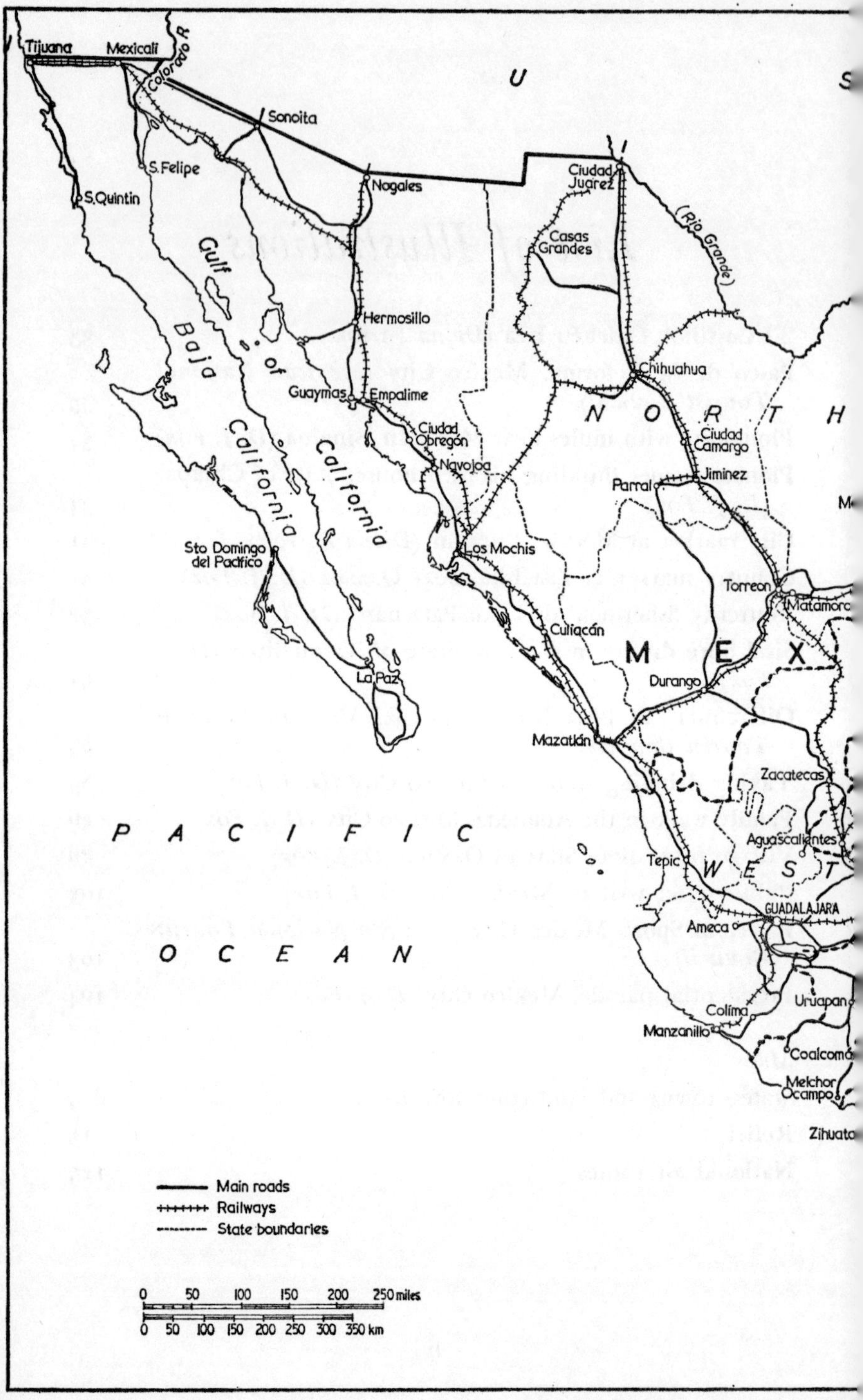

Tijuana
Mexicali
Colorado R.
U
Sonoita
S. Felipe
S. Quintin
Nogales
Ciudad Juarez
Casas Grandes
(Rio Grande)
Gulf of California
Baja California
Hermosillo
Guaymas
Empalime
Chihuahua
N O R T H
Ciudad Obregón
Navojoa
Ciudad Camargo
Jiminez
Parral
Sto Domingo del Pacifico
Los Mochis
Torreon
Culiacán
M E X
Durango
La Paz
Mazatlán
Zacatecas
P A C I F I C
O C E A N
Aguascalientes
Tepic
W E S T
GUADALAJARA
Ameca
Uruapan
Colima
Manzanillo
Melchor Ocampo
Main roads
Railways
State boundaries
0 50 100 150 200 250 miles
0 50 100 150 200 250 300 350 km

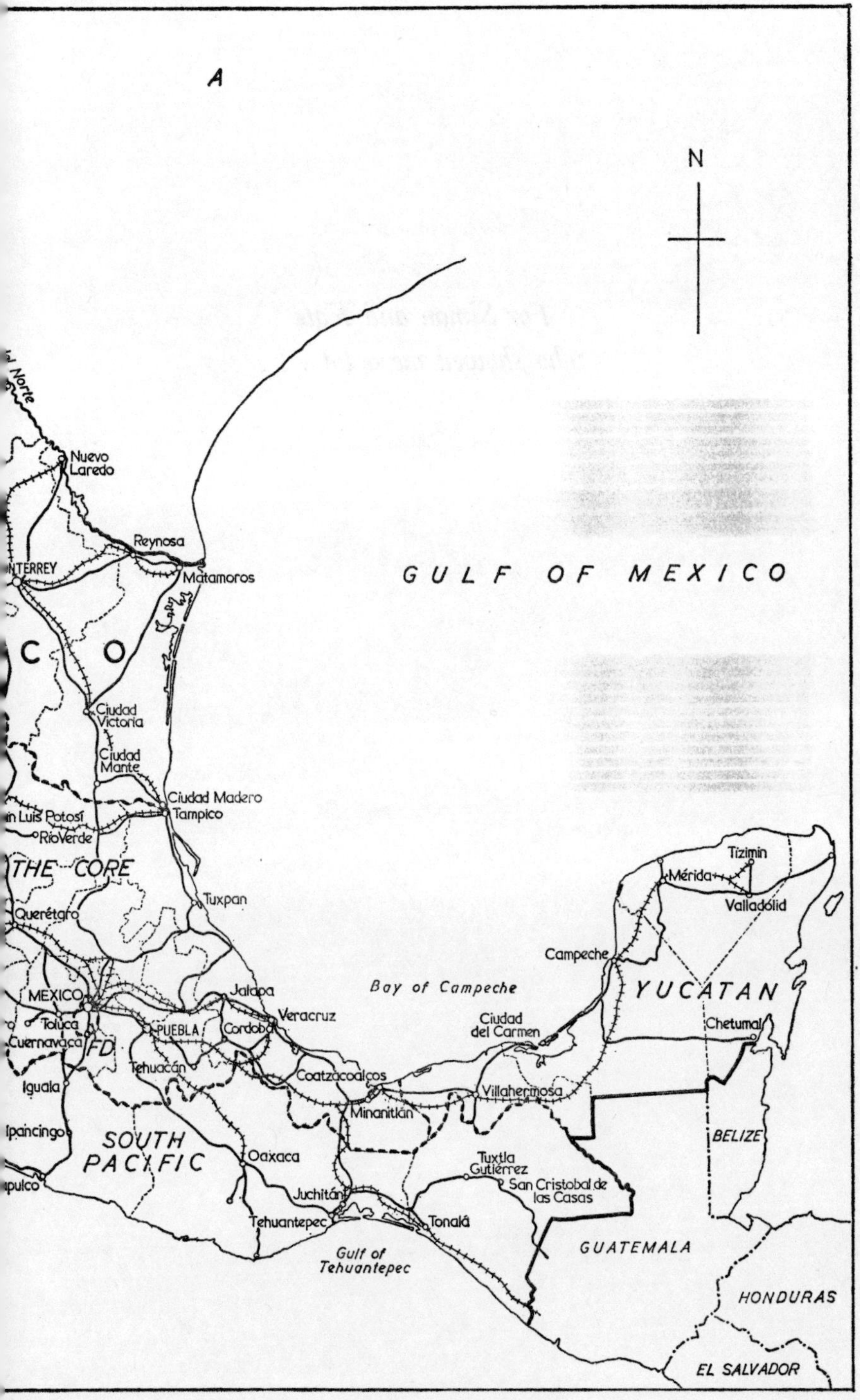

A
N
GULF OF MEXICO
Nuevo Laredo
Reynosa
Matamoros
NTERREY
C O
Ciudad Victoria
Ciudad Mante
Ciudad Madero
Tampico
n Luis Potosí
RioVerde
THE CORE
Tuxpan
Querétaro
MEXICO
Toluca
Cuernavaca
FD
Jalapa
Veracruz
PUEBLA
Cordoba
Tehuacán
Iguala
lpancingo
pulco
SOUTH PACIFIC
Oaxaca
Coatzacoalcos
Minanitlán
Juchitán
Tehuantepec
Tonalá
Gulf of Tehuantepec
Bay of Campeche
Ciudad del Carmen
Villahermosa
Tuxtla Gutiérrez
San Cristobal de las Casas
Campeche
Mérida
Tizimin
Valladolid
YUCATAN
Chetumal
BELIZE
GUATEMALA
HONDURAS
EL SALVADOR

*For Simon and Kate
who showed me a lot . . .*

I

The Country and the People

THE CONCEPT OF MEXICO

THE concept of Mexico, as we know it today, dates only from 1848. As the result of a war with the United States, the government of Mexico lost more than half of its national territory to its northern neighbour. Of this area, the states of Arizona, California, Nevada, New Mexico and Texas alone totalled more than 772,000 square miles (1,994,800sq km). Five years later, in 1853, the then government of Mexico sold a further strip of territory to the United States—the Mesilla Valley or Gadsden Strip—in order to build a southern transcontinental railroad.

Since 1853, therefore, Mexico has covered an area of some 758,000 square miles (1,944,561sq km)—a little bigger than the nine countries of the European Community plus Norway. As a federal republic of twenty-nine states, two territories and a Federal District, its official name today is 'The United Mexican States' (Estados Unidos Mexicanos). The more usual name, *México* (pronounced May-hee-co), derives from the language of the ancient Aztecs. The country occupies the southern part of the North American continent between 15° 13′ N and 32° 43′ N. To the north it is separated from the United States, on the east, or Texan side, by the Río Bravo, known in the United States as the Rio Grande, and on the west by the artificial frontiers of 1848 and 1853. To the south it is separated from the republic of Guatemala by the Suchiate river, and from Belize (British Honduras) by an agreed frontier based on the Río Hondo. To the east Mexico is bounded by the waters of the Gulf of Mexico; to the west, by the Pacific Ocean, into which projects for more than 500 miles the desolate peninsula of Lower California. In addition to this there are a number of small islands (totalling 2,071 square miles or 5,363sq km) off the coast, but these, although economically important in various ways, make up an insignificant proportion of the national territory.

The modern country of Mexico is the third entity to be known by that name. The first was the Aztec kingdom of Mexico, based on the city of Tenochtitlan, a lake city founded in the year AD 1325 which became the centre of a considerable empire of client states in the Valley of Mexico. In the fifteenth century through war and conquest this state spread north and south into the high uplands, the central plateau of modern Mexico. Nevertheless, even at its greatest extent, around the year 1480, it covered only a small proportion of the modern territory.

The second entity to be known as Mexico was the creation of the Spaniards, who arrived at Tenochtitlan in the year 1519, a small expedition under their celebrated leader Hernán Cortés. Cortés was aided in his annexation of the territory of Mexico by a considerable number of allied states who resented the pretensions of the Aztecs, and who feared in particular the appalling tribute in human sacrifice which they had to pay when defeated in battle. Having conquered the central Valley of Mexico, the Spaniards spread rapidly throughout the rest of the central plateau and within twenty years had explored far to the south, right down into the territory which is now Central America. The whole territory, including Central America, was placed under the rule of the Kingdom of New Spain; its capital, a new city built on the site of Tenochtitlan, was Mexico City. Throughout the colonial period the proper name of the kingdom remained the Kingdom of New Spain, but the name of its predecessor came increasingly to designate it in public usage, and when in 1821 the Mexicans proclaimed their independence from Spain their government controlled immense territory stretching all the way from Costa Rica in the south to present-day California and the mission settlements in the north.

This empire was perhaps too big to last. In its day, it was by far the largest single political unit in the world. But it is interesting to note that until the war against the United States in 1847–8 successive governments of Mexico, although divided as to how their country should be governed, were able to maintain substantially the independence and integrity of national territory. They lost, however, the territory of Central America in 1824 and that of the state of Texas in 1836, the secession of which was to be the ultimate cause of the war with the United States. They did not lose, as they might well have done, the territory of Yucatán, a peninsula which juts out into the Gulf of Mexico and until modern times was hard to reach by overland communications; and they only lost the territory of California as a result of military conquest by United States military forces.

To this day there are a large number of descendants of former Mexicans living in the southern and south-western parts of the United States. In Arizona and New Mexico in particular they form a substantial ethnic minority. Even in the more northerly state of Colorado as late as 1876 the state constitution provided for Spanish as a second national language. Today the Mexican-Americans, or *chicanos* as they are familiarly known, are increasingly conscious of their important cultural heritage. What has long been a superficial interest in the Spanish-American heritage in the United States has assumed a more serious and endurable form. Mexican-Americans living in the United States are important because of their relative financial affluence, and the support that they give to their families in their home villages. The pressure for present-day Mexicans to swell their numbers by illegally entering the United States to work as contract labourers (*braceros*) has been a continual bone of contention between the two governments, and one repeatedly discussed at presidential meetings. In modern times it has been considerably complicated by the question of smuggling, particularly along tracks from below the Rio Grande.

PHYSICAL CHARACTERISTICS

When Cortés was asked to describe what Mexico looked like to the Spanish court, he is said to have taken a piece of paper, crumpled it, and replied: 'That is Mexico.' The traditional story embodies the most important fact about Mexico's geography. Geologically the southern half of the North American continent was formed by collision with the southern continent in the age-long processes of continental drift. The mountain chains of Mexico, which run from north to south through the country, dividing it in two from side to side, are the product of immense volcanic forces thus released.

The highest of these mountains, Mt Orizaba, whose Aztec name, Citlaltépetl, means 'The Mountain of the Star', reaches a height of 18,700ft (5,747m), and its brilliant summit is visible in good weather from 100 miles out in the Gulf of Mexico. The snowcapped peaks of Popocatépetl (17,887ft or 5,452m) and Ixtaccíhuatl (17,343ft or 5,786m) dominate both the view from Mexico City and the travel posters.

Basically, there are three climates in Mexico: that of the mountains and the high mountainous plain above 6,000ft (1,830m), the *tierra fría*, is alpine in character and supports a vegetation of light pine forest shading off into the eternal snows of the great peaks. At the height of the plateau itself, a great raised block of land averaging some 6,000ft above sea level and which forms what geographers call the Core of Mexico, the climate is known as the *tierra templada*—the temperate country. Here the altitude moderates the tropical heat (the air is still thin but the region is pleasant to live

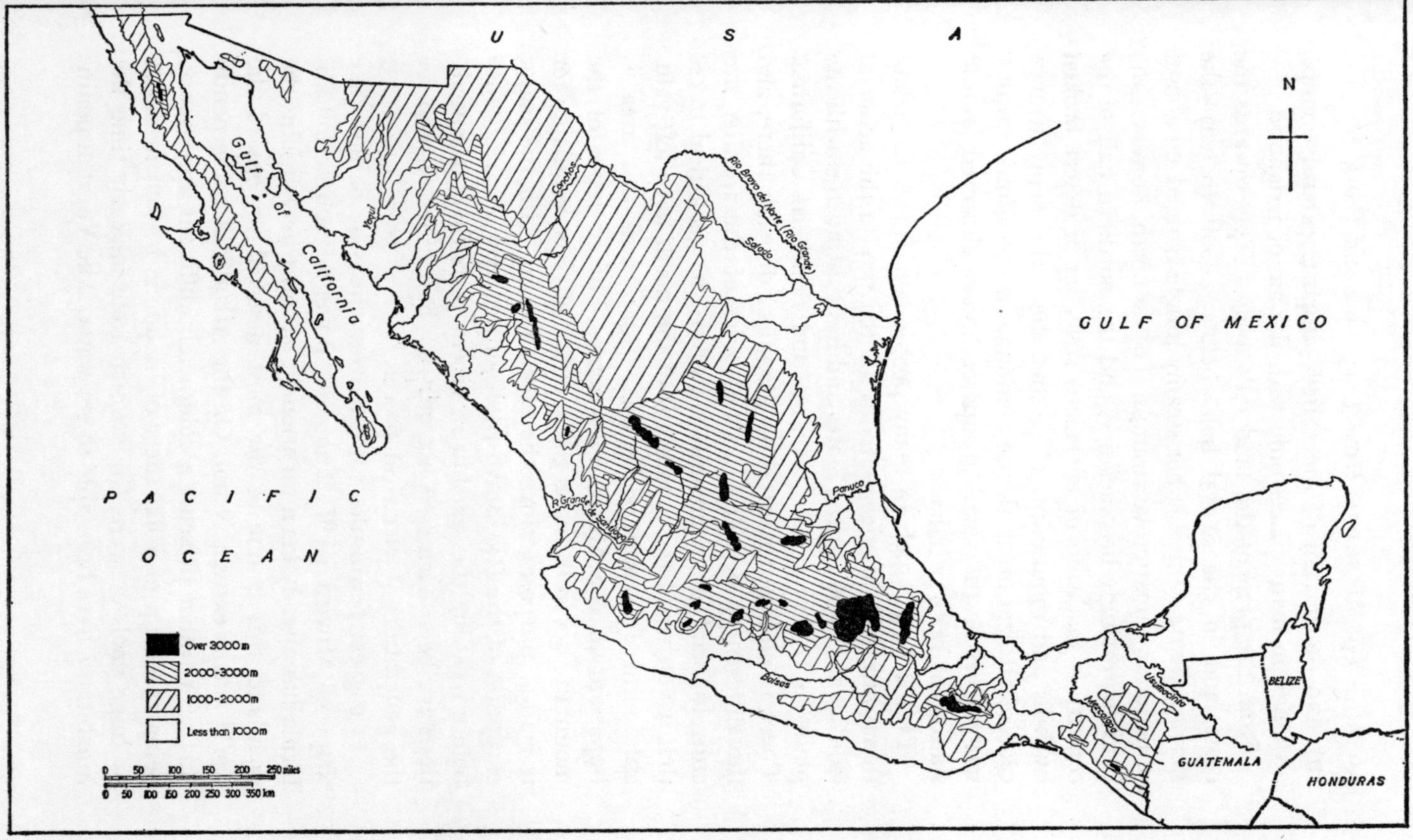

U S A
N
GULF OF MEXICO
PACIFIC OCEAN
Gulf of California
Yaqui
Conchos
Rio Bravo del Norte (Rio Grande)
Salado
Panuco
R. Grande de Santiago
Balsas
Mezcalapa
Usumacinta
BELIZE
GUATEMALA
HONDURAS
Over 3000 m
2000-3000 m
1000-2000 m
Less than 1000 m
0 50 100 150 200 250 miles
0 50 100 150 200 250 300 350 km

in), and the terrain of the valleys supports extensive crops, although in many places only with the aid of irrigation.

From the plateau the land falls away steeply towards the coast, and in the coastal belts below 3,000ft (900m)—the *tierra caliente*—there is hot steamy jungle fringed by almost impenetrable mangrove swamps. To the north, however, the land increasingly becomes dry, and the northern half of the country is made up of enormous stretches of desert broken by hills and mountains. Here and there the many strange cacti of all sizes break the desolation, as do occasional mining settlements or the small groups of houses clustered around stations or railway halts.

This desert, which to many people constitutes the traditional image of Mexico, extends all the way to the artificial frontier with the United States and has continuities with the plains of Arizona, New Mexico and Southern California. There is no sharp natural geographical division there, and the differences between the two sides of the frontier are entirely social and economic. However, the geological forces that have shaped the mountains of the north have left valuable mineral resources in their wake, and this area is important to the Mexican economy. The presence of the mountains severely limits the number of rivers available for irrigation purposes, since they tend to run, with the major exception of the Rio Bravo itself, only a very short distance before reaching the sea; but in recent years their potentialities have been harnessed not only for irrigation but also for the generation of electrical power.

Two great peninsulas jut out from the cone or horn-like shape of Mexico itself. The long finger of Southern California has already been mentioned; except where it joins the mainland this is one of the most deserted regions of the world and is extremely hot. On the Atlantic side the peninsula of Yucatán presents a completely different appearance, being made up of a flat sheet of limestone broken in places by huge pools or wells from which from an early time the inhabitants have been able to get water. The Yucatán peninsula on the northern part is covered with only a thin scrubby vegetation and shades off to the south-west into the *tierra caliente*, but its unique characteristics enabled it to become the centre of the mother civilisation of Central America and the one from which Mexican civilisation was eventually to derive, namely the Maya.

Today the Yucatán is not very heavily populated, and its maritime aspect makes it an agreeable climate in which to establish holiday resorts—that of the island of Cozumel off the coast of Yucatán is one of the most famous, and others are being developed. The climate of this area has much in common with that of the Caribbean islands or the peninsula of Florida which it faces.

CLIMATE

Although Mexico is a tropical country in its geographical situation, it will be seen that it contains within it at least three major climates. That of the *tierra caliente* is very hot all the year round, although somewhat moderated by the influence of the sea near the coast. It is divided climatically into a hot dry and a wet season. During the wet season it tends to rain in sudden bursts in the late afternoon or evening, and these downpours can be extremely heavy. During the 'dry' season there is, of course, much less rain and it is during the period from November to February that many people choose to visit Mexico when the climate is most favourable. The rainstorms also occur in the *tierra templada*, but there the climate is generally considerably cooler and it approximates to the Mediterranean. Temperatures are not generally extreme in any part of Mexico, however, with the exception of the northern desert, which, burning hot by day, can get extremely cold at night.

The problem is that all this area, with all its advantages of mildness and climate, is still desperately short of rainfall. Only in the zone of the isthmus of Tehuantepec, and on the Pacific coast of the state of Chiapas, is there sufficient rainfall

B

all the year round to sustain vegetation of a conventional type, and those areas are tropical in character and for geographical reasons difficult of access. The problem of the Central Plateau, therefore, is not that the wet season is too wet but that the dry season is too dry. It follows, that the land area of Mexico that is actually available for agricultural use is extremely limited—the best estimate is that only around 7 per cent of the total land area of Mexico is suitable in any way for arable cultivation.

VEGETATION

Mexico has an exceedingly rich and varied vegetation. The tropical districts are unusually well provided with varied species of brilliantly flowering plants, of which the poinsettia will be one of the most familiar. These flowers are pollinated by equally brilliantly coloured and variegated butterflies, and the total effect is one of great charm. The desert, on the other hand, provides Mexico with picturesque cacti whose strange stunted spiky forms so impress the visitor. In between them there are numerous smaller species, many of which are grown in pots the world over by people who perhaps neither know nor care about their origins. They are strange forbidding plants, of limited economic use; only one, the maguey cactus, is extensively used for economically valuable purposes. In times past its sharp leaves used to make fibres which were the basis of clothing, but today it is of greater importance as the source of the juice from which the fermented drink pulque is made. This powerful liquor is extensively used by the poorer Mexicans to help them drown their sorrows.

The basic reason why civilisation can flourish in Mexico to the fantastic extent that it has done, may be found in the interaction of three food plants, the virtues of which were discovered at an early stage by the inhabitants of Middle America (Mesomerica). The three crops are corn, or maize, which provides the basic staple-diet food, beans, which in traditional cultivation use the tall stems of the maize plant as the poles for their support, and squash. With them were cultivated also the chillies, which provided not only the hot, explosive quality characteristic of the Mexican cuisine, but also vital additional vitamin C. The three plants go well together in primitive cultivation and each used in conjunction with the others helps to provide a surprisingly well-balanced diet capable of sustaining human life for long periods without any further admixture.

THE PEOPLE

It is believed that the original inhabitants of Mexico arrived on the North American continent across what is now the Bering Straits, probably across a land bridge existing during the last interglacial period. From there they spread gradually down the west coast of North America and so southwards into the region which we now call the Core of Mexico. By 10000 BC they were already established in the southern part of the modern core region, where the climate was then somewhat cooler than it is now, capable of supporting not only a more varied vegetation, but also a range of small game suitable for a hunting community. After about 6500 BC the climate began to get warmer again, and the game migrated further north. The early Mexicans met this crisis by systematically collecting vegetable foods, and in time developed the cultivation of wild vegetable crops. The most important of these, which began to be cultivated around the year 5000 BC was, as has already been mentioned, corn or maize. By about 3500 BC permanent settlements of huts began to appear, and with the discovery of pottery, the medium for food storage, the groundwork was laid for the emergence of the first major Mexican civilisation in the region of the Isthmus of Tehuantepec. This is the civilisation which today the archaeologists know as the Olmec. It is the progenitor for all subsequent Mexican civilisations.

Ethnically, the peoples of Mesomerica, as it is known, bear a striking resemblance to the peoples of Eastern Asia, and they are, of course, of much the same general appearance as the plains Indians of North America. Their languages and cultural traits, however, have very little in common, and even in Mexico itself there are more than 360 languages spoken, although the vast majority of them are rapidly becoming defunct. Nor is there any comfort for those who regard the New World's pyramids and temples as evidence of cultural identity, for Mexican arts and architecture, too, appear to have developed from indigenous solutions to problems which all human beings have had in common. Much confusion, however, has arisen from the fact that the archaeological record is as yet still very imperfectly known. It is now certain that many of the features of Maya civilisation were already present in Olmec times, and the collapse of Olmec civilisation seems to have been due to circumstances of social unrest and even revolt rather than to, as was formerly believed, climatic change or exhaustion of soils.

Nevertheless, in the last 1,000 years BC there began to emerge in the southern part of the Yucatán peninsula a new civilisation which was ultimately to displace the Olmec, and whose language it appears to have taken over. This was the Maya which, once established, was to go from strength to strength and reach a peak in the classical age around about the year AD 400. To this day the huge temple complexes and monuments of the last age of Maya civilisation are an exciting and inspiring subject for the tourist, and the cultural achievements of this society were by any standards astonishing.

Politically, the Maya period was a collection of warring or another individual city. This civilisation was finally disrupted around about the year AD 900, when it was taken over and partially conquered by a related culture which had states, which from time to time fell under the sway of one developed in what is today known as the Valley of Mexico. From the name of their capital city, Tula, in the modern state of Hidalgo, this civilisation is known as the Toltec. The family resemblances which it bore to the Maya are very striking, and indeed the chief difference seemed to be the much greater emphasis on human sacrifice with the result that the recurrent wars which were a feature of the period became much more serious. The Toltec hegemony over the Core of Mexico was displaced by an even more militant warrior culture, that of the Aztecs, who called themselves the Mexica and so ultimately gave the name to Mexico itself.

So far none of the cultural changes or waves of migration had done much to disrupt the recurrent pattern of Mesomerican civilisation. The Spanish invasion, however, had an overwhelming and almost devastating effect upon it, out of which emerged the complex dual character of present-day Mexico.

The impact of the Spanish conquest was twofold. First of all, there was the fact of conquest and the cultural shock caused by the introduction of wholly new ideas and the subjection of the entire country to a unified organising and directing system of control. Secondly, although quite unintentionally, there was a tragic ethnographic collapse, caused by the introduction of unfamiliar diseases and the reduction of the population of Mexico by the combined effects of these factors to under a tenth of what it had been on the eve of conquest. The Spaniards, moreover, intermarried freely with the Mexicans, and so gave rise to a new racial grouping, those of the mestizos or people of mixed race. Today the mestizo forms the bulk of the Mexican population. They are new people who have inherited both Spanish and Mexican cultural traits, but who, because of the circumstances of their origins, have found it difficult to identify with one or other of their cultural inheritances. Like the descendants of Spanish families and all other Mexicans for public purposes, they speak Spanish.

Modern Mexico, therefore, is homogeneous in its variety.

The bulk of the population is mestizo. The descendants of Spanish settlers who have not intermarried with Mexican families, then, are very few in numbers, and certainly form well below 5 per cent of the population, although their numbers have been swollen somewhat by a heavy wave of Spanish immigration following the Spanish Civil War of 1936–9. At the other end of the scale, the Indians, as the Spaniards mistakenly named them, today number just on three million or 6·9 per cent of the population. They continue in many remote areas and even, such is the broken nature of the geology of Mexico, in some areas that are extremely close to the capital, to live in their traditional styles, wear traditional dress consisting of white baggy trousers, floppy hats and sandals and conduct their everyday lives much as their ancestors have done for the last 2,000 years or more. Although, as has already been said, the languages of Mexico are numerous, linguistic minorities do not form ethnic minorities as such, an important difference from the cultures of Europe or the Middle East.

CHIEF HISTORICAL LANDMARKS

By far the most important cultural contribution the Spaniards made to Mexico was the introduction of Christianity. Unfortunately, such was their fanaticism for the religion, honed and sharpened by generations of fighting against the Moors in Spain itself, that the immediate effect of it was the extirpation of the most important cultural manifestations of the ancient civilisations. The ancient books and records were destroyed, and the belated attempt of one or two of the more conscience-stricken Spaniards to try to record the historical traditions of the people whom they had subdued came too late to redress the balance. The result is that although today we know a good deal about the ancient civilisations, we still find it difficult to construct a precise and accurate history. This is ironic, for the Olmecs had succeeded in devising the most accurate calendar the world has known until modern times, and they and their successors, the Mayas, were obsessed with the precise dating and recording of events. Their temples and pyramids are enormous monuments in stone, covered with huge quantities of glyphs, symbolic characters of writing, recording events, dynasties, conquests, dates of foundation and restoration and so forth. The traveller who goes to the Yucatán peninsula, or who visits the ancient sites in Mexico, will therefore be well advised to gain some knowledge of the site before he gets there. The very names of the kings who ruled, and the military leaders who commanded the huge forces that created these monuments, are as yet only imperfectly known to us.

With the Aztec times our knowledge is more substantial. The accepted date for the founding of Tenochtitlan is AD 1325. There followed a series of eight rulers, kings of the Mexicans, the story of whose wars and conquests make weary reading; but the main pattern is straightforward enough. The conquests reached a peak under the rule of the Emperor Moctezuma I, who ruled from 1440 to 1469. His rule marks the apogee of the Aztec civilisation, and before he died the signs of collapse were already evident. His grandson Moctezuma II (1502–20) was still on the throne when the Spaniards came; he is the 'Emperor Montezuma' of Prescott's history of the Spanish conquest.

The suddenness and the completeness of the Spanish conquest has puzzled many generations of scholars. Some attribute it to the introduction of the horse as a means of transport, for the horse was previously unknown in America and the Aztecs had no beasts of burden—the enormous loads of the pyramids were moved and raised by the labour of men alone. Others have attributed it to a variety of external causes, particularly to the religion which the Spaniards introduced. To some extent, of course, this is true because Christianity meant the proscription of human sacrifice, and the Spaniards therefore received a great many allies who feared and hated the tribute of the Mexicans; but the disarmament of the Mexicans themselves arose from the religious traditions that they had inherited.

The Aztecs, like the Mayas before them, believed in the second coming of the god Quetzalcoatl, a fair-skinned, fair-haired deity, who would return from the east. The landing of Cortés was hailed by many of the wise men and seers of the kingdom as being the return of Quetzalcoatl, and it is clear that Moctezuma himself shared this view. He therefore welcomed the strangers to his city and accepted a great deal of what they had to say, eventually being killed himself by a flying stone when the people rose in revolt against the destruction of their ancient temples. Resistance to the conquest was subsequently co-ordinated on a hasty and improvised basis by his son Cuauhtémoc, who has become a national hero for many Mexicans. With his hasty execution in 1525 the resistance of the Mexicans in the Core area virtually came to an end.

It was, however, to continue for generations on the outlying frontiers of Mexico and the last punitive expedition against the Mexican Indians was mounted as late as the beginning of the present century. The history of this war has a great deal in common with that of the Indian wars of the United States—a history of repeated abuse of treaties and the struggle for poor land resources.

But the colonial period was not one of complete calm, despite the apparent stability of the three centuries of Spanish rule. Outbreaks of unrest and rebellion disturbed the peace in Mexico City itself, but the Spanish colonial system allowed for appeal against the decrees of the heavily centralised administration to groups of inspectors who came round at periodic intervals to hear grievances and to punish malfeasance in office. Nevertheless, the impressive thing about the period of colonial rule is that it lasted so long, and that during this time Mexico City was the capital of an immense province of virtually proverbial wealth. During the eighteenth century Spanish colonial administration itself was improved and brought up to date; prosperity increased, and a small but substantial middle class began to emerge.

Mexicans were not eager for independence and the development of modern Mexico was largely the result of fortuitous external circumstances coupled with the particular circumstances of the country. In the year 1808 the Emperor Napoleon invaded Spain and placed his brother on its throne. At one stroke the personal link of all the colonies in the Americas and elsewhere was severed from the government of Spain. The colonists were at a loss to know what to do. The rule of the colonies had been so tightly centralised in Spain itself that even the descendants of Spanish settlers had not been allowed to play any part in their own government. On the other hand, they were wealthy and powerful landowners, exercising the rights of a patron over a large number of Indians (*peones*).

The revolt for Mexican independence was touched off by a parish priest, Father Miguel Hidalgo y Costilla, who on 16 September 1810 called his small flock to prayer in the church at Guadelupe and proclaimed that it was time for them to rise against the Spanish oppressors. Faced with the prospect of an Indian revolt, the upper and middle classes joined together to suppress it, and the hesitancy of the leadership enabled it to be defeated easily. Father Hidalgo was captured, tried and condemned by an ecclesiastical court and executed.

His example, however, gave hope to others. One such man was Vicente Guerrero, who, from his mountain retreat, led a long guerrilla revolt against the Spaniards. At the same time political changes in Spain changed the situation drastically. In 1815 the war was over in Europe and the Spanish government was restored, but it proved extremely conservative and alienated its most liberal supporters. In 1820 they rose in revolt and seized control of the government of Spain itself. The new government's laws offended Conservatives in the colonies, and in 1821, under the leadership of a Mexican of Spanish descent, Agustín de Iturbide, they gave Mexico independence and proclaimed a separate kingdom. Since they had no king, after a short period of hesitancy, Iturbide proclaimed himself Emperor of Mexico, and ruled for almost a year before a combination of forces overthrew him. The liberals, who had achieved his fall, then proclaimed Mexico a republic, and, because of its enormous size, wrote a constitution for it (the Constitution of 1824) which was modelled on that of the United States, with a president, a Congress and a system of federal states. Iturbide attempted to revolt against the new government and was subsequently executed.

Mexico seemed set for a successful and prosperous future. But this did not come, largely owing to the spectacular but disastrous career of one man, General Antonio López de Santa Anna. He was president eleven times in Mexico between 1832 and 1853, and every time his natural indolence and inability to govern, as opposed to seizing power, brought disaster on his country. The secession of Texas, the disastrous war of 1847 with the United States and lastly the sale of the Gadsden strip all represented defeats for Mexico, the responsibility for which must be placed principally on Santa Anna himself. He was a brave man, and not a bad general, but he was worse than incompetent, he was unlucky.

The final fall of Santa Anna in 1855 brought about a severe reaction. The liberals had seized power, and they were determined that there would be no further conservative rule like that of Santa Anna. They saw in the church the chief enemy of progress. They proceeded to pass a series of punitive laws restraining his powers and reducing its influence in political matters, and these laws collectively are known as the Reform. Under the laws of the Reform the church properties were seized, the church was forbidden to meddle in politics and clergy could not hold political office. Considerable wealth would have fallen into the hands of the state had it not been for an unfortunate conjunction of events.

In the early years of the republic the infant state had had to borrow a great deal of money in New York in order to finance the debts inseparable from setting up a new government and political organisation. These debts had been prey for the speculators, and one of them in particular had succeeded in persuading the French government to take an interest in his case. The Emperor Napoleon III then sat on the throne of France. He was eager to emulate at low cost the success of his distinguished uncle, and he saw in Mexico the opportunity to carve out a new empire. Hardly had the liberals of Mexico finished fighting against the conservatives to establish the laws of the Reform, when they were faced with the news that French troops had landed in the harbour of Veracruz. Ostensibly they came to collect the debts due to the debtors; in practice, it soon became clear that they were there to stay, and a Habsburg prince, the Archduke Maximilian, was discovered who was prepared to sit on the throne of Mexico.

This was the short-lived period of the Second Empire (1864-7), which was only possible because the government of the United States to the north was then distracted by its own civil war. As soon as that war was over the hostility of the United States forced the French to withdraw. The empire collapsed, and Maximilian himself was shot on the Hill of Bells outside Querétaro in 1867.

The restored republic (1867-77) was a period of great intellectual distinction. It enjoyed the enormous prestige at its success in driving out the French, and its leader, the civilian lawyer Benito Juárez, president of Mexico from 1859 to 1872, has become a legend, both for the tenacity of his resistance to the French and for his distinction as a leader attempting to seek peace and secure a settled government in a turbulent country. When he died, however, it was the most distinguished of the military leaders against the French, Porfirio Díaz, who was to take over. Díaz, a successful leader and general at the age of thirty, finally seized power in 1877 and held it almost without interruption until 1911.

The age of Díaz was an era of strong centralised government in which a nominally liberal but in practice conservative government attempted to rule Mexico by inviting in foreign capital and giving it every incentive to bring to light the natural resources of the country. Authoritarian government promised sharp repression of any attempted revolt, but the fact that the country was weary of a generation of war gave the regime a head-start and in practice it met very little opposition. Only in the last five years of its rule, when the memories of the bad old days had become dim, did it become apparent that a major revolt was brewing against the government. The development of the country, the growth of a new potentially revolutionary middle class, and even the beginnings of workers' organisations were to combine to bring about the Mexican Revolution.

The Mexican Revolution refers to the period of Mexican history since 1910 when its first leader, the civilian, Francisco I. Madero, led a successful revolt against the octogenarian dictator, Díaz. Madero himself was assassinated in 1913 in the course of a military coup. However, the conservatives' attempt to put the clock back did not reckon with the widespread agrarian revolt which in the meantime had broken out under leaders such as Emiliano Zapata in the south and 'Pancho' Villa in the north. For generations the peasants had longed to redress the effect of the Spanish conquest and to recover the land for themselves, and at last they felt strong enough to do so. Between 1910 and 1920 more than a million Mexicans died in the course of fighting and from disease. The effect of the revolution was only slowly felt, although its immediate effect was the writing in 1917 of the Constitution under which Mexico is governed today. This Constitution was unique in including not just the formal instructions for the organisation of government, but a proclamation of the social goals for which government existed, in particular the rights of workers and the dominant role of the state in the creation, preservation and maintenance of economic resources.

At first attempts to put the Constitution into practice were hesitant, but with the presidency of Lázaro Cárdenas (1934–40), the Mexican government at last found itself in a position to deliver the legislation which both the workers and peasants had so long demanded and for which so many other people had also worked. Since 1940 Mexico has been governed by an orderly succession of presidents pursuing the policy of a single ruling party which seeks to embody the experience and the desires of the Revolution. There are many who say that it has not gone far enough, and in 1968, when the XIX Olympic Games were held in Mexico, there occurred a series of student demonstrations calling for the establishment of a new and more regular form of government, which gave rise to clashes with the police and many deaths. Since then, however, there have been signs that government is attempting to incorporate these new demands in its policies and to meet the changing circumstances of the 1970s, and everyone agrees the story of social and economic development in Mexico is by no means finished.

THE POPULATION

The upheavals of the Revolution, with its attendant outbreaks of typhoid and typhus, resulted in a drastic net reduction in the Mexican population—a decrease which was greatly accentuated by the arrival of the world influenza epidemic of 1918. The result was a net decline in population between the censuses of 1910 and 1921, a decline which was not effectively redressed until the 1940s. Since 1940 the Mexican population has grown with extreme rapidity, until in the 1950s it became the largest Spanish-speaking state in the world. The effects of this development are shown in Table 1.

The rapid rise in the population has been accompanied by a very high birth rate (43·7 per 1,000 in 1971) and a steady fall in the rate of infant mortality (now 63·6 per 1,000 live births), a fall considerably helped by the provision of central social services and universal medical care. The very high birth rate results in an exceptionally youthful population,

TABLE 1: AREA AND POPULATION OF MEXICO

State and capital	Area (sq km)	Population (1970)	Density (per sq km)
Aguascalientes (Aguascalientes)	5,589	338,142	60.50
Baja California N (Mexicali)	70,113	870,421	12.41
Baja California S (La Paz)	73,677	128,019	1.74
Campeche (Campeche)	56,114	251,556	4.85
Coahuila (Saltillo)	151,571	1,114,956	7.36
Colima (Colima)	5,455	241,153	44.21
Chiapas (Tuxtla Gutiérrez)	73,887	1,569,053	21.24
Chihuahua (Chihuahua)	247,087	1,612,525	6.53
Distrito Federal (México)	1,499	6,874,165	4585.53
Durango (Durango)	119,648	939,208	7.85
Guanajuato (Guanajuato)	30,589	2,270,370	74.22
Guerrero (Chilpancingo)	63,794	1,597,360	25.04
Hidalgo (Pachuca)	20,987	1,193,845	56.88
Jalisco (Guadalajara)	80,137	3,296,586	41.14
México (Toluca)	21,461	3,833,185	178.61
Michoacán (Morelia)	59,864	2,324,226	38.83
Morelos (Cuernavaca)	4,981	616,119	124.70
Nayarit (Tepic)	27,621	544,031	19.70
Nuevo León (Monterrey)	64,555	1,694,689	26.25
Oaxaca (Oaxaca)	95,364	2,015,424	21.13
Puebla (Puebla)	33,919	2,508,226	73.95
Querétaro (Querétaro)	11,769	485,523	41.25
Quintana Roo (Chetumal)	42,030	88,150	1.75
San Luis Potosí (San Luis P)	62,848	1,281,996	20.40
Sinaloa (Culiacán)	58,092	1,266,528	21.80
Sonora (Hermosillo)	184,934	1,098,720	5.94
Tabasco (Villahermosa)	24,661	768,387	31.16
Tamaulipas (Ciudad Victoria)	79,829	1,456,858	18.25
Tlaxcala (Tlaxcala)	3,914	420,638	107.47
Veracruz (Jalapa)	72,815	3,815,422	52.40
Yucatán (Mérida)	43,379	758,355	19.28
Zacatecas (Zacatecas)	75,040	951,462	12.68
	1,967,183	48,225,238	24.51

despite increased life expectancy and the consequent burden on the social services for the aged. The crude death rate in 1971 was 9 per 1,000.

At the same time the effect has been most noticeable in the rapid acceleration of Mexico's urbanisation. Urbanisation is not unusual for Mexico: the eighteenth century, too, was a period of rapid urbanisation, and Mexico had large towns and even cities before it had an urban industrial base on which to support them. The problems of feeding Mexico City were already acute in the eighteenth century.

Today, however, the most noticeable feature about Mexico is the enormous size of the capital itself. Mexico City in population is the third largest city in the world; in a population of some forty-eight million people, it and its surrounding metropolitan area contains over nine million, and in area and extent it is even more impressive, having outflowed not only its legal bounds in the Federal District but also having outpaced the natural resources available to support it. The second largest city in Mexico, Guadalajara, has a population of over a million, and 40 per cent of the population of Mexico, or 19.9 million, live in urban areas, defined as communities of more than 2,500 persons.

RELIGION

In colonial times, the church in Mexico was a co-ordinate part of government. It administered its own legal system, held its own courts and enjoyed special privileges within the state, such as exemption from taxation. It was an important civilising influence on the frontiers of New Spain, where a list of mission stations testify to the lonely life of the pioneers of Christianity in the wilderness. The most celebrated of these today is perhaps the city of San Francisco in the United States.

The association of the church with the conservative party, however, brought it into disrepute with the liberals in the early nineteenth century, and in view of the liberal role in the proclamation and establishment of a republic in Mexico, a collision was perhaps inevitable. The fury of the liberals was not let loose on the church until 1855, but from that date onwards a series of acts under the Reform deprived the church of a great deal of its wealth and standing within the community, and permanently removed its ancient privileges.

Under the long rule of Díaz, although the church did not regain its privileges it did regain something of its former respect, and by the beginning of the twentieth century was even beginning to receive the ideas of social progress implicit in the Catholic Reform Group of the later nineteenth century. Nevertheless, with the outbreak of the Revolution, the church was subject to violent attacks from most of the groups that supported the revolutionary cause. In the 1920s militant socialism was the order of the day. The church was severely restricted by a series of punitive acts, which, among other things, provided that priests might not wear their dress in public; that they could only exercise their mission if they were licensed to do so by the state; that the last vestiges of ecclesiastical property, including the churches themselves, would become state property and would be open to all at

---

The contrast of old and new:

Antique Mexico—'El Castillo', Chichén Itzá, with the Platform of the Tigers and Eagles in the foreground.

Modern Mexico—Paseo de la Reforma, Mexico City, with the Monument to Independence in the foreground.

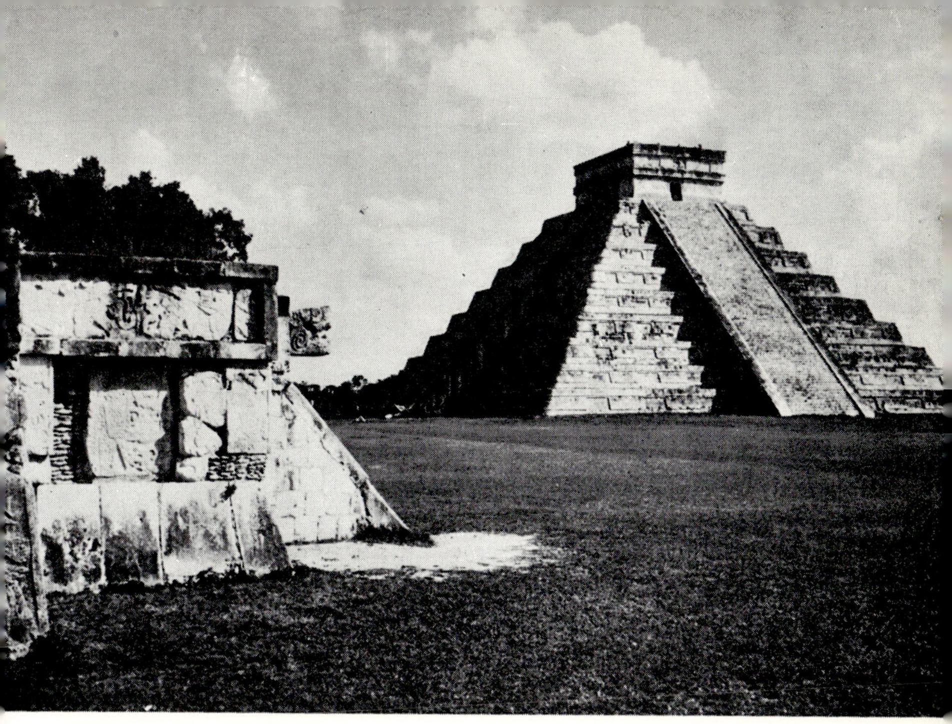

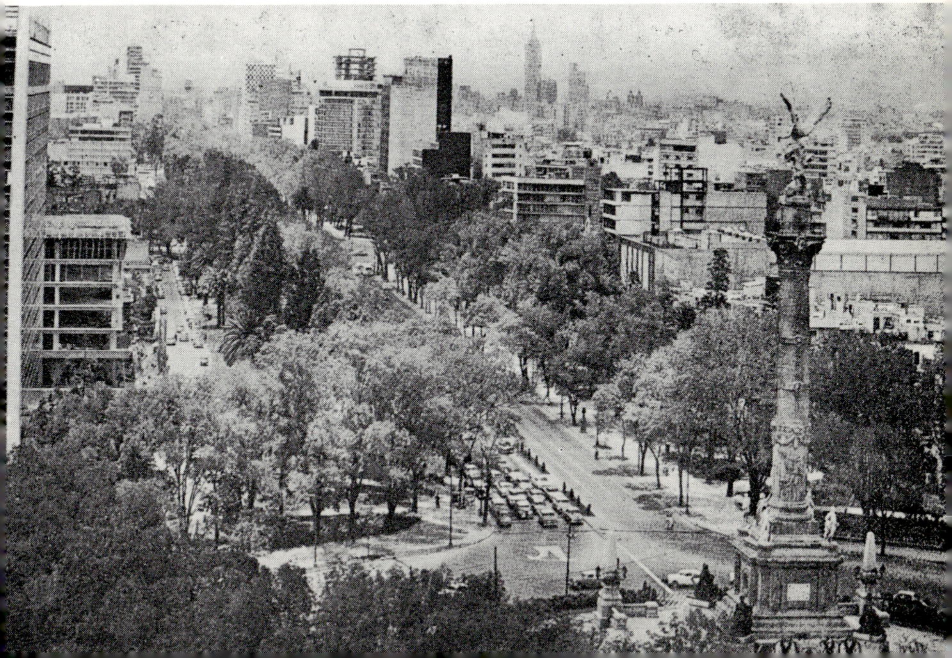

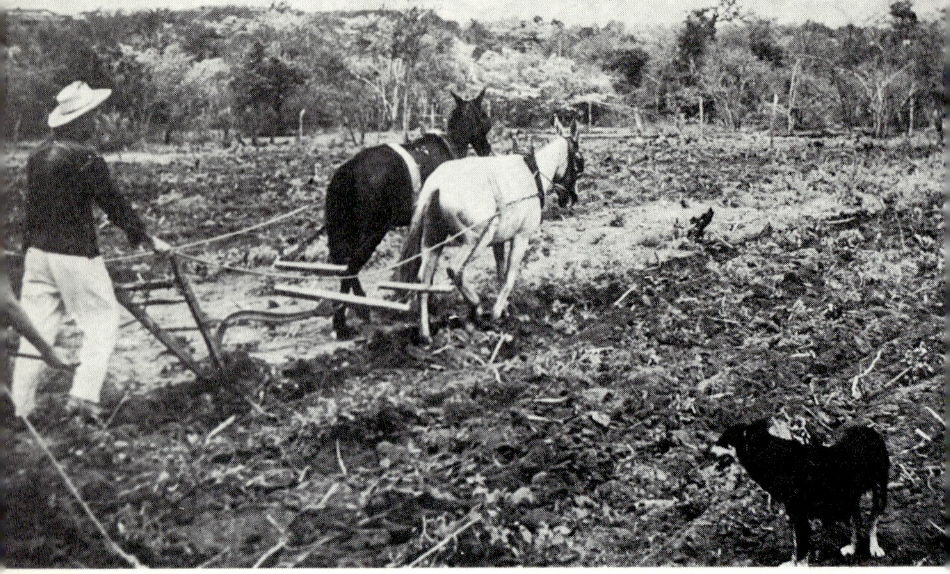

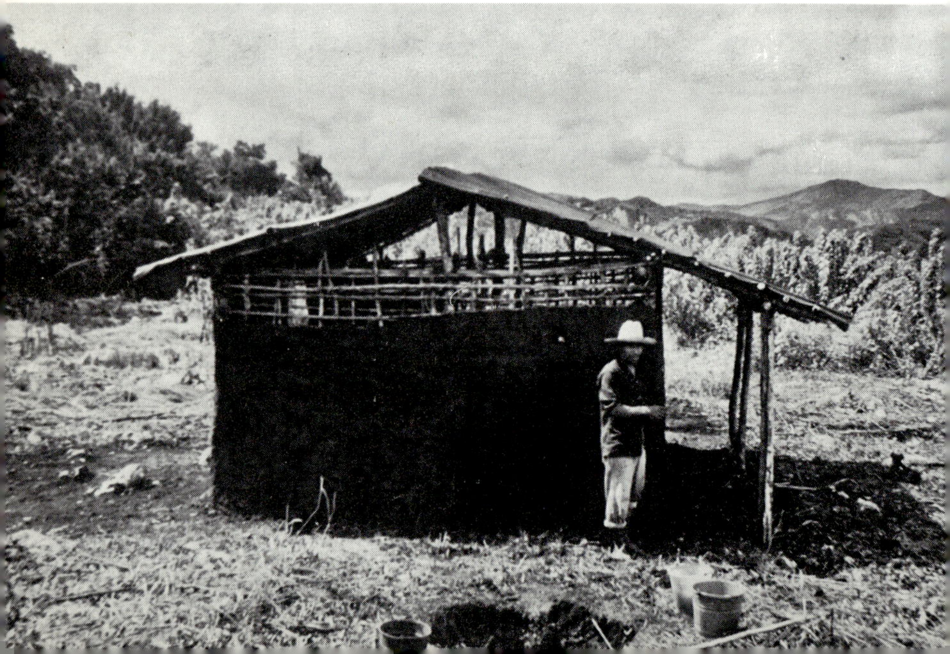

all times; that monastic institutions would be completely suppressed; and that the very number of bishops themselves should be limited to one for each state. Under the rule of Plutarco Elías Calles (1924–8), full-scale civil war broke out between partisans of the Catholic cause and fanatical atheists, in which the government joined in the suppression of the clerical revolt, particularly in the state of Michoacán. An attempt was even made to set up an autonomous Mexican Church. However, no one would attend its services.

Eventually in 1926 all of Mexico was placed under an interdict. For the first time since the Spaniards arrived in 1519 no church services were held anywhere in the country. This continued for three years, until, with the mediation of the then American ambassador, a truce was arrived at. It was an uneasy one, and did not give way to real peace until in 1940 the newly-elected president announced that he, too, was a believer.

Today the laws against the church have been much relaxed and the Mexican hierarchy consists of ten archbishops and thirty-eight bishops. At the census in 1970 98·8 per cent of the population were reported to be Catholic—not all of them practising, particularly among the poorer classes.

Opening up new lands for cultivation is hard work:

Ploughing with mules near Mazatlán, Sinaloa.

A pioneer farmer building his own house, State of Chiapas.

There are few avowed freethinkers and, despite years of earnest proselytisation, only a very small (876,879) Protestant community in Mexico. The Jewish community numbered 49,181 in 1970.

THE LANGUAGE

Spanish is the official language of Mexico and is spoken by all educated Mexicans. It is the sole medium of instruction in the country's schools, and the second language most often taught in them is English.

Nevertheless, as has already been indicated, the other ancient languages of Mexico do still survive in their regional settings. Náhuatl, the language of the ancient Aztecs, is still spoken by nearly 300,000 as their sole language, and is known to many others. The language of the ancient Maya is still the sole tongue of some 80,000 people, and related linguistic structures, culture and customs are evident in many remote areas, where vestiges of the language still survive for use in local purposes. In 1970, 1,104,955 persons were reported who spoke Indian languages only.

The Spanish spoken in Mexico is distinct from Castilian largely through its use of a large number of native and foreign-loaned words. In structure it has not altered very much. The fact that it is primarily a language of the educated class means that there are relatively small regional differences in the way that it is spoken, although there are enough still to be noticeable, obviously relating to the intonation characteristic of the original native languages.

NATIONAL CHARACTERISTICS

Like other nations influenced by Hispanic modes of behaviour, the Mexicans are a society built tightly around the extended family unit. To this day the houses in which they live bear a striking resemblance to those of Spain itself, being built round courtyards, with only barred window openings to the outside world. Family feeling is extremely strong, and the network of family relationships is extended by the Hispanic custom of regarding one's *compadres* (fellow-godparents) as members of one's extended family.

Traditionally a male-orientated society, the public life of the Mexican revolves around the café and in particular around the market square where the male members of different families meet to exchange conversation about every matter under the sun. Outside the large cities, and even in the large cities, a less-rigid conception of time exists than is common in the Europe of the post-railway age. One does not apologise for being late until one is up to half-an-hour overdue for an appointment, unless the time has been specified as *hora inglés* (English time), in which case punctuality is intended.

This loose conception of time has given rise to some extraordinary caricatures of Mexicans, notably that they are slow and unreliable. As to the first charge, they are evidently cheerful and gregarious, and a Mexican crowd is a lively and not-too-serious assembly. The Mexicans have a great capacity for enjoying themselves and an attractive habit of picking up the pleasing customs of other peoples. Thus, for example, they have adopted the *mariachis*, or characteristic band of the Veracruz area, from French invaders. Their public parks are broken by attractive areas of colour where the balloon-sellers stand just to display their wares. They have shown a great zest and enthusiasm for the best features of modern architecture, both of which flourish with incredible vigour in the fertile artistic soil of Mexico. The amount of energy that has gone into the expansion and development of the modern industrial sector of Mexico, too, effectively refutes the charge of unreliability; it would be impossible to run a society of this degree of complexity were it not sustained by a very effective, and indeed punctilious code of mutual trust.

2
The Capital and the Regions

THE broken character of Mexico's natural environment has posed great barriers to expansions. The characteristic which is most noticeable about its social structure is the existence of the *patria chica*, or 'little fatherland'. The area that means most to the individual is not Mexico as a country, nor even his home state (for the state is very frequently an artificial entity, whose boundaries have been extensively altered in the search for political stability). No, it is the valley in which he lives, in which he is separated from the outside world by high mountains, and by the spirit of localism and local pride which is strong in Mexicans, who point with great joy and enthusiasm to the great men of their country that have been born in their own local areas. A great many of these men, too, were born in very small communities, some of them so small that they do not even appear on any but the largest and most detailed modern maps.

Nevertheless, geography insists that Mexico also has a larger regional pattern, and this has to be taken into account when governments attempt to plan for any area larger than a local valley. Climate and geology conspire to ensure that Mexico is, possibly permanently, afflicted with the most intense inequalities in regional development, and inevitably people have looked more and more to the central government to redress their inequalities. Consequently, today there is a real sense in which every Mexican looks first to the national government after his own locality, and the regional variations tend, with some historic exceptions, to be very much less important.

THE CAPITAL

Any discussion of regional variations in Mexico must begin with the capital, for the country is the product of the capital and not vice versa. In theory, Mexico City is a federal capital situated within its own district, the Federal District, which is administered on behalf of the president by a governor appointed by him. Juridically this is true, but in practice Mexico City has long since outgrown the boundaries of the Federal District, although there is an area in the south which it still has not completely filled. The greater metropolitan area of Mexico City, now the third largest city in the world, overflows in particular into the state of Mexico. The state of Mexico is only one of a number of tiny states, with, however, relatively large populations, which cluster in and around the capital, but are nevertheless distinct from it by the nature of the governmental system as much as by the nature of the terrain itself.

When Cortés planted his capital on the site of Aztec Tenochtitlan in 1519, he did so for political and not economic reasons. Otherwise he would never have chosen to build his capital on the site of a lake city, which had been built up on piles in the middle of water. The result is that as Mexico has continued to expand, and the stone buildings of the conquerors have spread outwards from the centre, so the ground underneath the capital has begun to sink. In places the buildings are more than 16ft below their original level, and sometimes, as in the case of the cathedral of Mexico City, below ground level. This sinking has been greatly accelerated by the need for an expanding city to consume the water resources of the area. The draining of artesian wells has resulted in an acceleration of land subsidence and in turn it has given rise to an acute drainage problem, for Mexico City, which is situated in a valley completely surrounded by mountains in the middle of an area that was formerly a lake, has a great deal of difficulty in disposing of its surplus waste.

The third major problem to afflict the city today is that of pollution. The high altitude, coupled with the numerous small motor-cars which speed along Mexico City's broad and splendid streets, have resulted in a permanent canopy of smog, and the effect of arriving in Mexico City from the air is to descend through a lid of pollution over the bowl in which the city lies.

Like all Mexican cities planned by the Spaniards, the heart of the capital is the main square or *Zócalo*. It is surrounded on one side by the cathedral, on the next by the National Palace where the presidential offices are situated, on the third by the Municipal Palace or seat of city government, and on the fourth by a range of attractive shops which extend downwards in the direction of the central park or Alameda. This area is the smart shopping centre of Mexico City, and corresponds roughly to the old colonial city; among its buildings there still remain a number dating back to colonial times which give the visitor an idea of what the capital of New Spain looked like in those days.

Beyond the Alameda two enormous boulevards intersect. These are the product of the French influence brought by the Second Empire and extended in the time of Porfirio Díaz, when the model for all public Mexican building was the French Second Empire style. These two great avenues are the Paseo de la Reforma and the Avenida de los Insurgentes. Both of them are splendid processional ways, six lanes wide, intercepted at intervals by roundabouts or traffic circles (*glorietas*), each with its appropriate monument. In this part of Mexico City is the diplomatic quarter and also the Mexico of the affluent tourist; the best hotels, the travel agencies and the offices of the principal airlines.

The Paseo de la Reforma runs up to the great knoll of rock on top of which stands the castle of Chapultepec, with the park of Chapultepec stretching around it in all directions. This park is the great recreation centre of the city. In colonial times the hill, which bears the name that the Aztecs gave it when they found grasshoppers there, was the residence of the viceroy, and for a hundred years it was also the residence of Mexico's presidents. Here the ill-fated Emperor Maximilian and his empress walked on the flower-decked terraces, and here President Madero learnt the news of the insurrection which was to overthrow him. Since 1934, however, Mexico's presidents have chosen to live in modest style in a small house in the park, and today the castle of Chapultepec is a museum.

To the east of the Paseo de la Reforma there is a large area where the streets are all named after European cities, and here, amid the improbable names of Nice, Liverpool and Hamburg, is the fashionable modern shopping centre of Mexico. Beyond this again stretch the best residential districts, mostly to the south of the city, while to the west and north there stretch out a ring of enormous satellite cities joined to the main bulk of the city by the principal bus routes. Transport is today a major problem for the capital, as will be seen later.

THE CORE

The Core consists of the central plateau of Mexico. On the north it is bounded by the desert, and to the south it falls away steeply towards the isthmus of Tehuantepec. It occupies slightly more than 17 per cent of the land area of the country. Geologically, it is the product of intensive vulcanism, which has not only distinguished it by magnificent peaks and majestic views, but has covered the valley floor with a deposit of smooth ash which is very fertile. The result of this and the temperate climate is that the region as a whole (including the capital) contains over half the population of the country, stretching from Aguascalientes in the north-west as far as Vera Cruz, on the Gulf, which strictly speaking lies in the tropical lowlands but has gained its importance as the chief port for the Core region.

Politically, this area is divided into eleven states and the Federal District. The reasons are largely historical—all this area has been heavily urbanised since colonial times, largely as the result of the Spanish policy of planting settlements as a basis for cultural diffusion. In the eighteenth century the process was accelerated by the development of a secondary centre of settlement to the north of the capital in the valley region around Querétaro known as the Bajío, where copper mines formed a centre of economic activity. Each major town and its hinterland formed a separate state on independence, with further fission occurring for political reasons in the first fifty years after 1810.

Because of the intensity of settlement, as well as the nature of the longitudinal mountain ranges of the Sierra Madre which hem it in, communications in Mexico are heavily, although not exclusively, centred on the capital.

The climate, being moderated by altitude rather than latitude, is equable, but nights tend to be cold all year round. Mexico City itself has an annual temperature range of only some 10° F (5° C). Average temperatures in the cool season, between November and April, are in the mid-50s F (c 12° C), and the climate dry and sunny. In the summer it is warmer, but the rainy season beginning in June brings tropical rainstorms of sometimes torrential intensity. Annual rainfall in the Valley of Mexico itself is between 20 and 30in (500–750mm), which is far from sufficient for the needs of the dense population, and the capital is having to look further and further afield for better sources of water. Intensive cultivation enables Mexico to support the population largely on its own resources, but the total productivity of the region certainly falls well short of the proverbial wealth of Mexico, and the government is clearly unwilling to encourage further expansion but not yet able to offer any very compelling alternative.

A major problem here is that productive industry, as well

as population, is overwhelmingly concentrated in the capital, to an extent almost unmatched among the world's great cities. In fact before 1940 there was very little significant industry anywhere else that was not the primary production of minerals. Owing to the climatic and geographical difficulties, however, such schemes for relocation of industry depend on the availability of Mexico's scarcest resource—water—and hence the government since the 1930s has favoured what has become known as the 'river basin approach'. Starting with the Papaloapan Valley in the state of Veracruz, corporations were established to develop river valleys basing their efforts on dams for generating electrical power and supplying local settlements.

THE WEST AND SOUTH PACIFIC STATES

The Mexican west consists of the three states of Jalisco, Colima and Nayarit, together with the southern parts of the states of Sinaloa and Durango, which for statistical purposes are usually treated as part of the north. Before the Spanish conquest, these areas were largely uninhabited. In consequence, they were largely populated by Spanish settlers and to this day have a much larger proportion of farmers owning their land than other parts of the country.

The two northernmost of the three South Pacific states, namely Guerrero and Oaxaca, have much in common with the west. Geographically, they both consist of a thin coastal strip, very narrow—less than 3 miles (5km)—and discontinuous, which is cut off from the rest of the country by the Sierra del Sur. This is a rugged and wooded mountain range, with little level ground. It is excellent terrain for guerrillas, and it is not at all surprising to find that many of the historic figures of Mexico's heroic past come from these regions.

Jalisco shares part of the central plateau region and is economically well developed. It is here that has grown up Mexico's second largest city, Guadalajara, with a population (1970) of 1,196,200. It is a thriving and up-to-date city with a well-developed modern shopping centre, but retains as its focus its fine park and cathedral, as well as many attractive Spanish-style buildings. It is the regional centre for the west, too, which since 1927 has been linked through it with the capital by the Ferrocarril del Pacífico. The completion of this rail link, which was attended by considerable engineering difficulties, brought into the life of the republic the state of Nayarit, which had been administered as a Federal Territory throughout the nineteenth century.

South of Guadalajara, however, there is no land link with the states of Guerrero and Oaxaca. In fact, it is not even easy to get from Guerrero to Oaxaca—routes running from the capital to the former by way of Cuernavaca and to the latter by way of Puebla. One consequence is that there is a sharp social difference between these two areas which makes them economically distinct, as well as politically and socially separate from the west, or, for that matter, from the central plateau. The south of Mexico is the place where the Indian cultures and languages not only originated but survive to this day most strongly.

This is not a very productive area, nor has it very many substantial towns, and the only ones which the tourist is normally likely to visit are Oaxaca itself, famous for its pottery and blankets, and Acapulco, the playground of the rich, which is in itself cosmopolitan. The road to Acapulco, however, passes through some of the most evocative names in Mexico: Cuernavaca itself, in the heart of Zapata's territory; Taxco, in the mountains of Guerrero where are the great silver mines which for so long supplied Spain with an imperial treasure which it frittered away on wars in Europe; Chilpancingo, where the first Constitution of Mexico was written. The state of Guerrero itself is named after the Indian hero of Mexican independence, who later became briefly though tragically the president of his country. Oaxaca is the homeland of the great Benito Juárez and of Porfirio Díaz. Both were of Indian descent. Without the south the unique character of Mexico could not exist.

Geography has protected the old Indian cultures, but it does not give them many advantages. The principal one stems from the higher rainfall of the Pacific slopes, between 30 and 40in (750–1,000mm) annually. Soils are fertile, but there is a great shortage of agricultural land and farming is mostly of the subsistence type. The climate of the isthmus region, which Oaxaca shares with southern Veracruz, is tropical lowland, hot and humid rainforest, and until modern times extremely unhealthy in which to live and work. Chiapas, beyond the isthmus, is a highland state which, once under independent administration, decided to stay with Mexico and not to join Central America. Economically it benefits not only from a savanna vegetation suitable for stockrearing, but also from fertile mountain slopes where in recent years the cultivation of coffee and cacao has developed rapidly. Tuxtla Gutiérrez, the state capital, is the last major city before the Guatemalan frontier.

YUCATÁN

The Yucatán peninsula contains the states of Tabasco, Campeche, Yucatán, and the former Federal Territory of Quintana Roo (named after the hero of Yucatecan independence). It is the home of the bulk of the Indian population of modern Mexico and together with it, the south as a whole contains some 20 per cent of the entire population of Mexico in a roughly equivalent area. But geologically the Yucatán peninsula is quite different. It is a limestone lowland with a karst topography which has in places literally been undercut by the sea and, like the peninsula of Florida in the United States, it projects into the Gulf of Mexico.

Although the Yucatán peninsula enjoys a good annual rainfall of between 30 and 40in (750–1,000mm), the northern part is in fact semi-arid. This is because most of the rain occurs in the months from June to October, and because of the limestone structure it drains away quickly. Mayan civilisation was based in Yucatán on the occasional occurrence of large wells or *cenotes*, around which settlements could gather, and of which the Sacred Well at Chichén Itzá is the most famous. The Spaniards brought windmills, and by raising water from the subsurface, created new possibilities, represented by the attractive and largely unspoilt city of Mérida, the capital of the state of Yucatán.

The sparse vegetation of the northern plains is broken at frequent intervals by the large cultivations of *henequén*, whose sharp spiny leaves furnish the sisal of commerce. Southwards the occasional patches of forest become denser until all signs of human activity are wholly obliterated. Yet among this dense jungle, which stretches on into the Petén department of Guatemala and into Belize (British Honduras), lie the ruins of vast Mayan ceremonial centres, their buildings split by tree roots and their temples crumbling in the tropical dampness.

THE NORTH

The north today is only a fraction of the immense territory once ruled from Mexico City. Geographically it consists of the Northern Plateau (Mesa del Norte) which is a continuation of the Great American Desert which lies principally within the modern territory of the United States, and it covers almost a third of the land area of Mexico. Rainfall is almost everywhere under 8in (200mm) a year, and often much less. What vegetation there is consists of xerophytic shrubs and coarse grasses. Cultivation is only possible where there is irrigation, and as there are few permanent rivers and those only near the sea coast, the greater part of the agricultural production of this region consists of stock-rearing. This is, therefore, the land of the Mexican cowboy (*charro*).

It is bordered on the west by the Sierra Madre Occidental, the spine of Mexico, and a continuation of the Rocky Mountains. Here there are minerals, notably copper and iron, and despite the formidable heat and difficulties of transport these have long attracted attention. On the east the branch of the Sierra Madre Oriental which divides the Northern Plateau from the Gulf coastal lowlands, attracts sufficient rainfall to make the southern part of its foothills feasible as a site for agriculture. It is in this area that Mexico's third largest city, Monterrey, population (1970) 830,000, grew up. It would be in any case an important road and rail centre, but also benefits from the neighbouring iron-ore deposits which make it Mexico's most important steel centre.

Near to it, to the west, is Torreón, an important junction and copper centre. Across the mountains, on the coast of Tamaulipas, it is again hot and humid. Here lie enormous oil and gas reserves from which, with the Veracruz and Isthmian oilfields, Mexico is able to satisfy more than 90 per cent of its energy needs. Here in the north, rainfall, which is over 100in (2,500mm) in the Isthmus of Tehuantepec, is much less—about 35in (900mm) at Tampico, and the vegetation has thinned out to a tolerable level. Like the southern parts, however, this section of the Gulf coast is unpropitious for shipping and subject to the risk of violent hurricanes at unpredictable intervals.

BAJA CALIFORNIA

The peninsula of Baja (Lower) California, 750 miles (1,205km) in length, is a continuation of the Sonoran desert and hence of the Great American Desert, which it closely resembles. Geologically it is separated from it by the gulf of the Colorado river, the major part of which lies in what is now the United States. Although mountainous, it attracts under 5in (125mm) of precipitation annually, and because it is a peninsula there are no rivers on it to serve for irrigation. Hence it is, and is likely to remain for the foreseeable future, largely desolate, but there are occasional mining settlements for such improbable minerals as copper and onyx.

Nevertheless, the state of Baja California which occupies the northern part of the peninsula is one of Mexico's fastest growing industrial regions. The reason is that where the peninsula joins the mainland, there is a small patch of land around Mexicali on the frontier with the United States which can be irrigated from the Colorado river itself. This region, which is geographically a continuation of the Imperial Valley of Upper California, is fantastically productive and its truck-farming industry has boomed under the forced influence of the insatiable appetite of the large cities across the border. Mexicali itself, a shanty town of unprepossessing appearance, has grown out of all proportion on the profits of legal (and sometimes illegal) cross-border trade.

In recent years La Paz, capital of the new state of Baja California (South), has been linked to the northern productive area by a road which runs through some of the most barren countryside in the world. Hitherto it had been dependent for communication with the rest of Mexico entirely on the ferry service from Mazatlán in the state of Sinaloa, a regional centre for its immediate hinterland, like other Pacific coast ports, and there primarily for mineral exports.

THE GULF REGION

The states of the Gulf region, although each linked economically directly to the central economy, can also be looked at as a geographical unity with a character of their own. This is the true *tierra caliente*—mile after mile of tropical rainforest broken by stagnant lagoons and fringed for almost its whole length by sandbars which impede navigation without offering much protection from the elements.

The northern part, the state of Tamaulipas, is characterised by oil production, both in the north around the small port of Matamoros, and more importantly around the port of Tampico, 7 miles (11km) up the Río Panuco, which is fringed by oil refineries and storage tanks.

Vera Cruz, not the capital of the state of the same name, is a small city with a population of 242,000 (1970). Economically it has always been significant as a port, but until the present century was an unhealthy place to live. In 1914–15 it served as Mexico's capital during the occupation of Mexico City by the agrarian insurgents, and it was here that the programme of agrarian reform was first adopted by the revolutionary government of President Carranza. However, in earlier times, it was the scene of some of the most unhappy episodes in Mexican history: the landing of the Spaniards in 1519, of the Americans in 1847 and 1914, and of the French in 1848 and 1861.

Extensive sugar cultivation is carried on in its hinterland, and Tamaulipas as a whole was traditionally characterised by large estates, now broken up. The southern, isthmian region of the state, although once the seat of the Olmec culture, in modern times has been comparatively sparsely populated. In the time of General Díaz it was used as a penal settlement. The adjoining state of Tabasco, scene of some of the most bizarre episodes of the Revolution when it was ruled by a socialist governor who pursued a policy of militant atheism, is largely Indian in population, and the main crops in this relatively flat region are sugar cane, bananas and coconuts.

MEXICANS ABROAD

For many years now, Mexico has been a country in which people from less-fortunate countries have taken refuge, and not one from which its inhabitants have felt socially obliged to leave. Therefore, Mexico contains a surprising number of foreign residents. Many of them were or are refugees from Franco's Spain, or from other Latin American countries where currently they are not welcome. In the past, Mexicans from the upper classes used to complete their education in Europe, and many still do, but a very much larger number nowadays study at American universities, particularly those of California and the south-west.

The possibility of saving sufficient capital to become an independent proprietor or landowner in a few years, lures many poorer young Mexicans to the United States to work as contract labourers (*braceros*). This traffic was legal but strictly regulated by the United States government until 1965, when the previous agreement expired. Since then, as at times in the past, the pressure has been so great that the smuggling of illegal immigrants ('wet-backs'—from the supposed fact that they had swum the Rio Bravo) has reached major proportions. One of the first acts of the Nixon administration, and one that was bitterly resented by the Mexicans, was to order an intensive search of all people entering the United States from Mexico in case they might be smuggling drugs; listening devices were also installed in the soil along the frontier. Such actions cause great harm to the system of the exchange of working people, which is actually of great economic benefit to the United States as well as to the individuals concerned.

It is less well known that in addition to the many United States citizens who are of Mexican descent by virtue of the conquest of the territories in which they live, there are over $1\frac{1}{2}$ million first-generation Americans of Mexican stock, and

---

The market place is the centre of special activity in town and country:

City market at Mérida, Yucatán.

Country market at Zaachila, near Oaxaca.

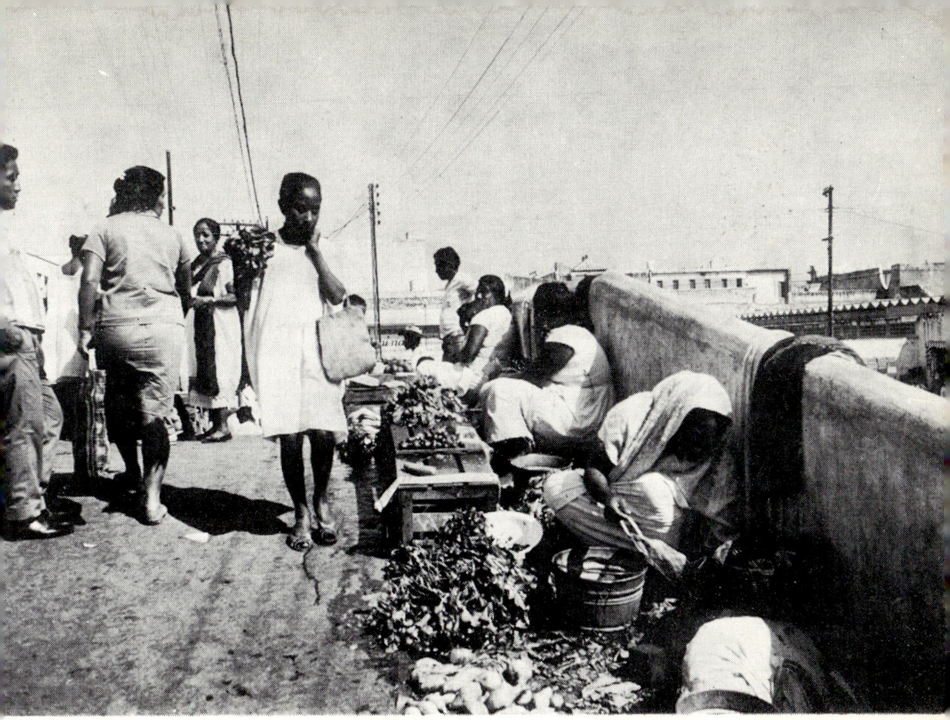

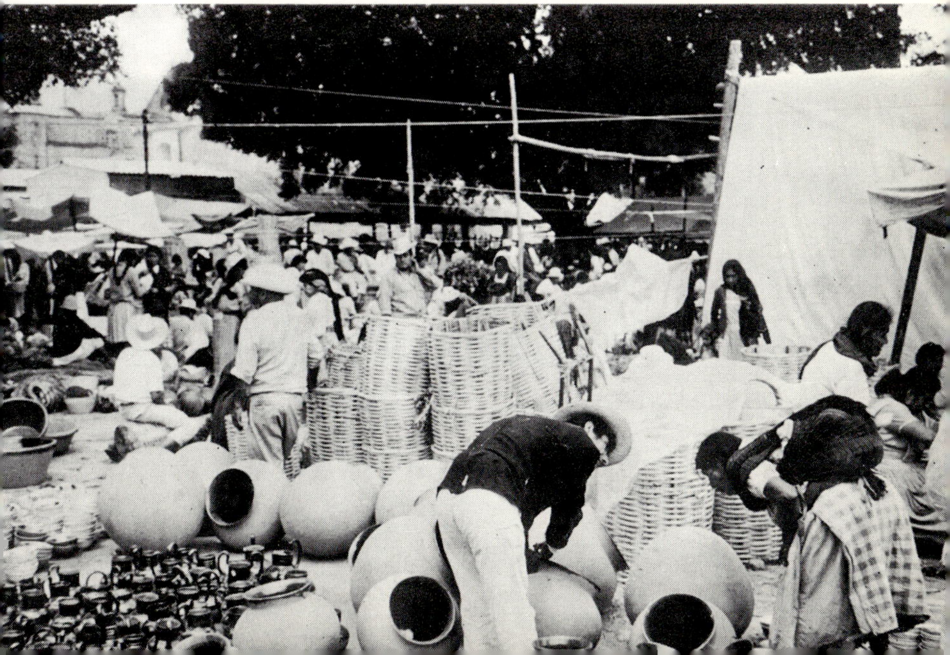

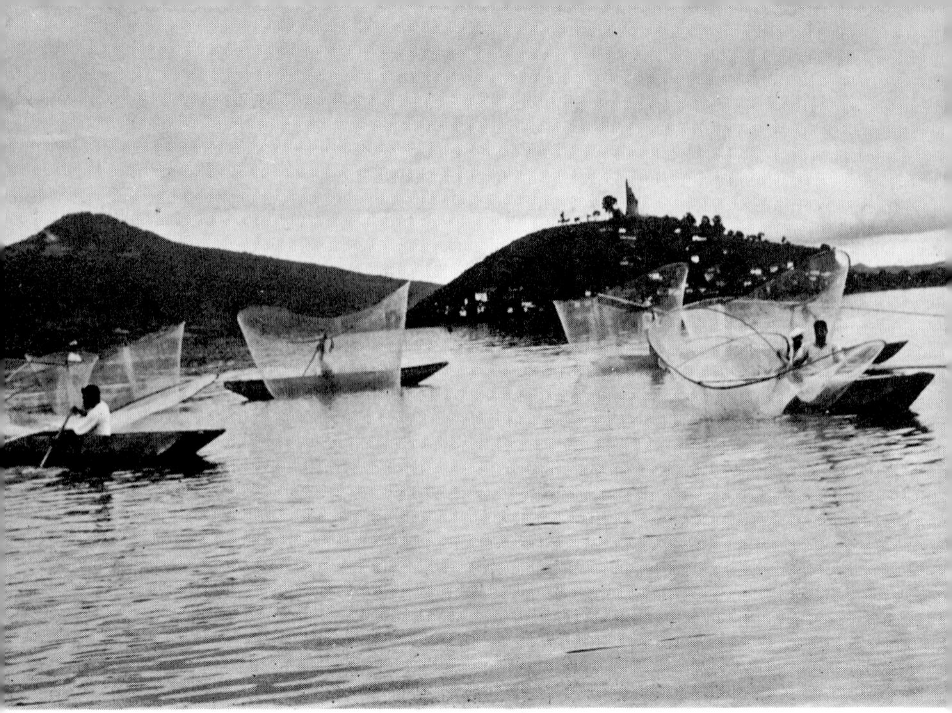

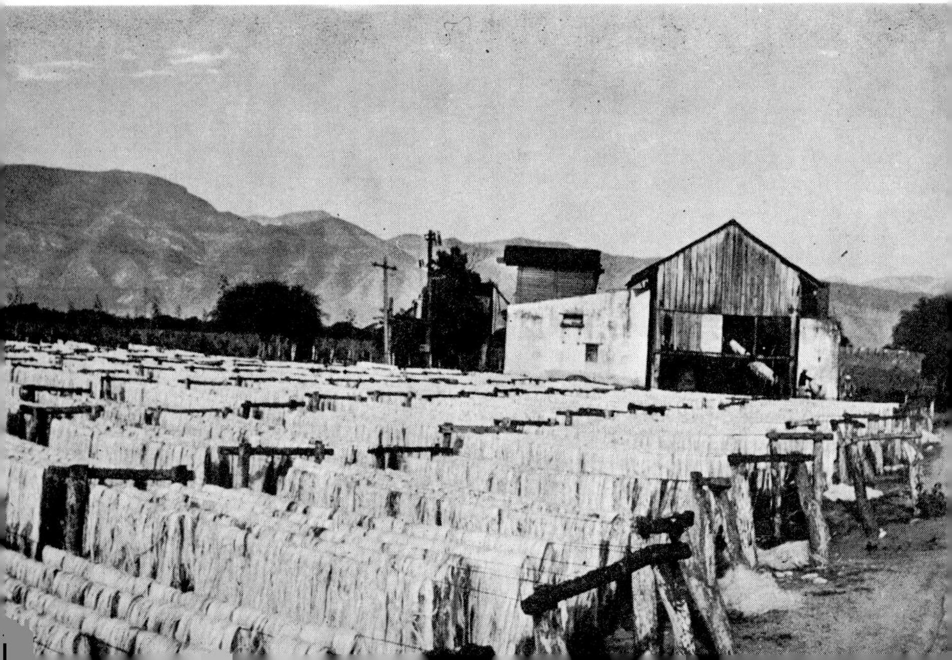

in 1969 there were more immigrants to the United States from Mexico than from any other country, namely 44,623. In recent years the *chicanos* have become, like other ethnic minorities, an organised pressure group, and are demanding attention in their own right.

In the south, where the frontier with Guatemala and with Belize (British Honduras) is virtually unmarked, Indian tribes who do not recognise the existence of modern frontiers move backwards and forwards with considerable freedom; but when some guerrillas tried to take advantage of this to form a secure base on the Mexican side during the guerrilla warfare in Guatemala in the 1960s, they were quickly located and dispersed by the Mexican army. As with other Latin American states, Mexico recognises rights of reciprocal citizenship with Guatemala under an agreement made under the auspices of the Organisation of American States.

Not all hard work is picturesque:

The 'butterfly fishermen' of Lake Patzcuaro.

Henequén (sisal) fibre drying in the sun, state of Tamaulipas.

3
How the Country Is Run

MEXICO became a federal republic for the first time in 1824. It was the form of government adopted in the nineteenth century by most of the larger Latin American states, and it is not surprising, therefore, that it was to this form that the country returned again in 1853. The interruption of the Second Empire apart, which is regarded by Mexicans as being a wholly alien regime imposed upon them from outside, the form of the federal republic has not been seriously questioned since and in 1857 it received its constitutional embodiment in the form of a written document. Its purely political provisions to this day remain the essential basis of Mexican government.

The first seven years of the Revolution (1910–17) saw a confused and haphazard succession broken into a number of very short-lived governments. At one period the country was in an almost complete state of anarchy, and efforts to draw it together again by calling a general convention of revolutionary chiefs proved to be more interesting to the historian than to the political scientist. Nevertheless, it was out of this broken period of experiment that there emerged the revised Constitution of 1917. Today this Constitution is more than just a written document under which Mexican government is organised, it is a written symbol of the bargain under which the victorious revolutionaries undertook to implement the social and welfare provisions for which their followers had fought.

THE CONSTITUTION

The Constitution of 1917 is a long and intricate document, shaped in a convention but ultimately the work of a team of brilliant lawyers working under the general direction of the conservative president Venustiano Carranza (1917–20). Carranza had been a state governor in the time of President Díaz, but had become an early supporter of the Revolution, and his caution and hesitation enabled him to survive the ruthless purging of the country's rulers by the military coup of 1913. Carranza's forces were known as the Constitutionalists. Under this umbrella were fought a great many different groups owing allegiance to different leaders, and certainly the most famous of these groups were the agrarian bands of Pancho Villa and Emiliano Zapata. The fame of these groups, however, is misleading, for the Revolution was not merely a movement for the distribution of land to peasants. It included also a large number of men who fought simply for constitutional reform, and yet others who fought for the precepts and promises of socialism in all its various guises.

It was only after the Constitution had come into effect that many of the provisions which these men had written into it were really appreciated for what they were, and their appearance in the Constitution itself is the product of the compromise necessary for a document to be accepted by so many different groups of supporters. Nevertheless, the survival of this Constitution, which is now the second oldest in use in Latin America, speaks well for the talent of the lawyers who drew it up, among whom the most famous is the name of Luis Cabrera. Cabrera and his colleagues based their work securely upon the structure of the Constitution of 1857, which in turn had been based in the main on that of 1824. This continuity goes far to explain the basic stability of Mexican government today, for it is securely rooted in the nation's traditions stretching back to colonial times.

First of all, the Constitution is based firmly upon the structure of Roman law inherited from the Spaniards. The judiciary, although protected by law, enjoys no special guarantees, and has no special role in the interpretation of the Constitution. Instead, it is accepted that it is for the politicians to make any changes that may be necessary, and for the lawyers to carry out the written work to the letter. Therefore, the document that is the Mexican Constitution goes into considerable detail in spelling out its provisions, and these provisions in turn are amplified by lengthy codes of legislation in which detail is very precisely stated.

Secondly, the Constitution recognises the diverse and disparate nature of the Mexican territory by establishing the federal system, but in order to retain control over it at the same time strengthens the part that central government can play as against those of the states. There are, therefore, no separate state constitutions as such and all must follow a model established at the centre, and the taxing power rests heavily with the central government, of which all the subordinate entities are thoroughly dependent.

Thirdly, the Constitution establishes the detailed provisions, among others, for the rights of labour, for the assurance that the land, its resources above and below the soil, both expendable and replaceable, will be vested in the state, and the use of the land will be subject only to the approval of the interests of the state. By this, therefore, the Mexicans have succeeded in checking the unrestrained exploitation of their mineral resources which they consider has been a feature of the development of other parts of the world and which to a great extent was encouraged in their own country in the time of Díaz.

The first government set up under the Constitution of 1917 was that of Carranza himself. In 1920, the president attempted to nominate his successor, but the man that he chose was both too mediocre and too unpopular to command any support, while his principal general, General Obregón, was clearly the next in line to succeed. As a result of a military revolt Carranza was overthrown, and in the course of fleeing, he was killed. A provisional government was established, which held elections as a result of which Obregón was returned to the presidency. This revolt of 1920 was the last successful revolt against the Mexican government. Since that time Mexican presidents have succeeded each other in orderly progression by constitutional means, and the last unsuccessful attempt to revolt against the Mexican government on any scale was crushed overwhelmingly in 1958. Given the nature of the Mexican countryside, and its revolutionary traditions, it is not surprising that there are still one or two small guerrilla groups operating in the rural areas. Despite the demonstrations of 1968, however, there is little doubt that the present Mexican government enjoys the support of the overwhelming majority of its population, and that the demonstrators themselves sought in the main to reform rather than to replace the present system.

The Mexican government of today is extremely powerful and centralised, and has very little organised opposition. In consequence, its administrative acts on occasion appear to be rigid and unimaginative and it is undeniably true that the control of promotion within the system is vested firmly within the party which has guided the destiny of the country since 1928. As we shall see, however, it is not necessary to draw attention to the considerable achievements of the party in maintaining economic growth despite an enormous expansion in population and increase in demand for every kind of natural resource. There are in fact few countries in the world in which such a high proportion of the ruling élite is so young; and even if the regime is élitist it is at least subject to constant deliberate change.

The reason for this lies in the provision of the Constitution for which the original revolutionaries of 1910 fought and died. This is that no elected officer, up to and including the president himself, should be permitted to hold office for more than one term. In consequence the entire ruling élite of Mexico has to undergo a general change of office every six years at the most, and a man or woman who wishes to rise within the system has to give satisfaction to his political supporters at frequent and regular intervals.

THE PRESIDENT

At the apex of the Mexican political system stands the president. The president is elected for a term of six years, and during that time he is in supreme control not only of the executive branch but of the entire structure of Mexican government. He makes all the principal appointments, is responsible for the preparation of the budget, prepares all legislation for approval by the Congress as well as a whole host of government regulations and ordinances, and in addition through his control of the party machine he is the ultimate authority in the choice of nominees for all executive positions. He is therefore very much more powerful than, say, the president of the United States.

Nevertheless, there are considerable limitations to his power. The most obvious ones are that he is only one man, who, however well served, can only pay attention to a certain number of things at a time, and by inclination, therefore, each president tends to pursue a programme of his own, by which his presidency is marked off by those of his predecessor and his successor. A curious effect of this is that since Mexican presidential nominees are chosen by the incumbent president acting together with the ex-presidents and certain other key officials, there has emerged a distinct alternation in office between representatives of the 'left' and the 'right' within the 'revolutionary family' to which 90 per cent or more of all Mexicans belong.

Again, the president is at his most powerful for the first two years of his presidency. In the middle two years he is primarily concerned with administering the legislation which he has introduced and seen passed in his first two years; in his last two years of office the fact of his existence becomes rapidly overshadowed by the burning question of who is to be his successor, and although the presidents in general succeed in holding back the question of a successor to the last possible moment, they cannot escape the loss of power that comes with the approach of the end of a term of office which is not renewable.

Lastly, Mexican presidents take office at a relatively early age. Since the revolution several of them have assumed their responsibilities in their thirties, and the majority of them in their forties. The result is that when a man leaves the presidency he still has a number of years of active life ahead of him, and since the time of President Cárdenas (1934–40), this fact has been conveniently utilised by employing the services of ex-presidents in important positions, such as guarding the destinies of state corporations, or as ambassadors abroad.

The president is assisted by a cabinet, which, like the American cabinet, consists of a number of secretaries directly responsible to him. Each is separately responsible for the conduct of his own department. The cabinet, as a collective body, has merely a ceremonial importance. The individual members of it, however, are very important, the more so since for the last thirty years it is from their ranks that the presidents have been chosen. The most important position, next to that of the president, is that of secretary of *gobernación* or interior. He is the president's right-hand man in the internal government of the country, and it is he who has the ultimate responsibility for the internal security of the state.

In theory, the secretary of external relations takes precedence over him, but in practice since 1932 Mexico has pursued a consistently neutralist foreign policy—recognising other countries on the basis of their existence and without regard to their ideological origins, completely eschewing any form of interference in other countries' internal affairs, and pursuing a relatively inactive policy even at the United Nations. This traditional posture of neutralism derives, of course, from Mexico's close proximity to the United States and the importance of that country in the world's affairs. It was well illustrated by the fact that during the period of the boycott of Cuba by the other American states, Mexico alone continued to maintain diplomatic and commercial relations with that country. Recent Mexican presidents have tended to take the conduct of foreign affairs onto their own shoulders, and have pursued a line strongly hostile to the domination of the world system by the great powers. They have been active in encouraging inter-American co-operation, although, since Mexico is separated from the south of America by the small group of Central American states which are strongly under United States influence, it is naturally rather difficult for Mexico to play a leading role in Latin America even if it wished to do so.

Mexico has no vice-president. In the event of the demise of the president, it is the secretary of external relations who would succeed to the presidency *ad interim*. Like the president, he would in that eventuality have to fulfil the stringent conditions of being both a Mexican citizen and the son of Mexican citizens, over thirty-five years of age, and not a member of the ecclesiastical estate. Mexico, with its socialist heritage, still retains the strongly anti-clerical features of the Constitution of 1857. The absence of formal religious duties, however, still means that the president has a strenuous ceremonial round, for he is required by custom to travel during his term of office, as in the period of campaign for his election, to every part of the country to show himself to as many of its citizens as possible. For the longer distances this will be done by air; for the shorter ones in a convoy of buses, accompanied by various local dignitaries and other officials to whom he can give the task of answering the many petitions which he receives on these occasions.

THE RULING PARTY

There is nothing quite like the ruling party of Mexico anywhere else in the world. The Congress Party of India is perhaps the nearest parallel, but there are many important differences. In 1928, President Calles (1924-8) was to have been succeeded by ex-President Obregón, running for a second term in defiance of the slogan of the revolution prohibiting the re-election of presidents. Despite this, he was in fact re-elected, but within days of his election he was shot at a victory banquet by a fanatic. The idea of an official government party, therefore, was partly the brainchild of President Calles, and partly that of his successor President Emilio Portes Gil (1928-30), who was responsible for its first statutes. The Party of the National Revolution (PNR), as it was then known, was a truly government party, for it was financed by a levy on the salaries of members of the government, and the purpose of it was to maintain unity among the supporters of the revolution and to enable them to maintain their control on the political system.

There were, at that time, three main bodies of support for the government. First of all, and most importantly, there was the army. Secondly, there was the force of the workers in Mexico City and the principal towns who had been formed into trade unions in the course of the fighting for the revolution, and who now exercised a powerful control on the main means of economic production and communications. Thirdly, there were the peasants, who at this period had still not, in their opinion, received any of the real benefits of revolution. President Portes Gil was a lawyer and a representative of the peasant movement, and his selection reflected the shifting in the balance of power that enabled this group to take its place alongside the other two in the formation of a new party.

Under President Cárdenas (1934-40) the government party became a powerful instrument of the incumbent president, who, by extending governmental intervention into every aspect of the national life, created an enormous federal bureaucracy which gradually supplanted the army as the representatives of government. In 1938 the party was reconstituted as the Party of the Mexican Revolution (PRM), and in 1946 it assumed the name it bears to this day, the Party of the Institutionalised Revolution (PRI). In the course of these changes the military became part of what is known today as the Popular Sector of the party, and a special organisation was created to look after its interests. Its withdrawal from politics was further symbolised by the choice of a civilian president in 1946, and since that time all Mexico's presidents have been civilians.

The party today is, however, divided into three sectors, and the other two sectors are those of the peasants (CNC) and of the organised workers (CTM) respectively. These sector organisations, like the organisation of the Popular Sector (CNOP), are organised throughout the republic and at each level of government from municipal to federal; their organisations interlock at each level with the committees of the party itself, and neither the workers nor the peasants can operate independently without the support of a substantial sector of their rivals. The membership of each of the three sectors is something in the region of two million, according to official figures, but as a great many members are inactive —counted as members simply by virtue of their occupations —it is very difficult to tell how many members of the political party are actually active. What is certain is that the party as an organisation for the choice of candidates and the maintenance of the political power is extremely effective, and that the central organisation enables each section of the official support of the party to receive its share of attention in turn.

OTHER POLITICAL PARTIES

There are, however, other political parties in Mexico. The major opposition party is the right wing Party of National Action (PAN). PAN is the party of the private sector of business, even though this sector is represented before the government by the chambers of commerce and trade which are counted as part of the ruling party. It also receives a considerable measure of support from Catholics who are unhappy with the traditionally secular tone of Mexican government itself, and therefore find it difficult to support a party which officially represents that government. On the left, there is a small Marxist socialist party known as the Popular Socialist Party (PPS), the creation of the labour organiser Vicente Lombardo Toledano. There is even a small splinter party of some of the older members of the revolutionary party who feel that the modern institutionalised revolution has failed to stand for its original principles, and these term themselves the Authentic Party of the Mexican Revolution (PARM).

The problem for each of these parties is that its support is not only very small but is thinly spread throughout the nation. Given the single-member single-ballot system used in Mexico, as in the US and the UK, it is very hard for any of these parties to obtain enough seats to reach power even on a municipal level, although two municipal parties which have shown a habit of municipal rebellion against the central government in electing opposition parties have been Hermosillo in the state of Sonora in the north on the one hand, and Mérida, the capital of Yucatán in the extreme south, on the other.

No opposition party has succeeded in gaining control of a state legislature since 1928, and even the Party of National Action has had difficulty in returning more than four or five members of the Chamber of Deputies. This has been rather embarrassing to the PRI, since it has always had and continues to have the pretensions of being a democratic party in a state in which opposition is freely allowed to operate. In fact, political opinion can be freely expressed in Mexico, and opposition newspapers and journals are free in their criticisms, while political organisation occurs on a widespread scale, particularly in support of left-wing splinter groups. Nor, despite occasional local excesses of enthusiasm is there any widespread tampering of the ballots in order to keep the ruling party in power; its dominance is so complete that it has been a long time since anything of this sort was necessary at all.

Accordingly, in 1962, the government, much embarrassed at the failure of the opposition to perform credibly, introduced a unique law to encourage its membership in the federal legislature, and by this law enabled the opposition parties to be represented in proportion to their voting strengths provided they had achieved 5 per cent of the vote or more. In 1971 this act was further revised to lower the threshold of representation and to increase the number of representatives. Mexico, therefore, is unique in the degree of encouragement given to its opposition, and the system for the choice of the Chamber of Deputies in practice somewhat resembles that of West Germany, being a semi-proportional system. It is notable, however, that the system has not been extended to the Senate, which remains solidly dominated by the PRI, nor, much more importantly, to the state governorships, where the real political power in the provinces lies.

THE ELECTORAL SYSTEM

The electoral system of Mexico, apart from the provision for proportional representation in the Chamber of Deputies, is similar to that employed in Great Britain or the United States, namely the winner takes all. Elections for president are conducted on the basis of the number of votes cast and there is no electoral college as in the United States. Boredom with elections is widespread and considerable effort has been made at recent elections to encourage a higher turnout at the polls.

When looking at Mexican voting figures in relation to population, however, it is important to remember the extreme youth of the Mexican population, caused by its rapid growth. In addition, many young people coming up to voting age seek work in the United States and may be out of Mexico for long periods of time. Women were given the vote in Mexico for the first time in 1952, but they play a more important role in politics than this would indicate for Mexico is one of the most enlightened Latin American states in the representation of women in the higher levels of government and administration.

THE LEGAL SYSTEM

There is no separate state judiciary in Mexico. The legal system is unified, although it is organised on the basis of the natural administrative divisions. At its head is the Supreme Court. The twenty-one members of the Supreme Court are appointed by the president with the consent of the Senate and, like other judges, they may be removed from office by the president for misbehaviour with the majority support of both Houses of Congress. This provision reflects the revolutionary belief that the judges ought to be both servants of the state and accountable to the people; an attempt in 1929 to make judges irremovable from office was reversed by President Cárdenas in 1934.

Under the Constitution of 1917, as under that of 1857, the Supreme Court was a single chamber on the model of that of the United States. The growth of business resulting from the complex litigation that developed as a result of revolutionary legislation, however, led to it being subdivided into three chambers (*salas*) in 1928, dealing respectively with civil, criminal and administrative law. In 1934 a special *sala* was added to deal with labour questions, and in the post-war period the continued growth of business resulted in the addition of an extra one to handle the cases that the others could not manage. The twenty-one judges are appointed for life.

At the same time five circuit courts were established in order to handle cases of lesser importance, and in 1954 a sixth circuit court was formed to handle cases arising in the Federal District. Today there are eleven, all primarily concerned with appellate jurisdiction, and the bulk of the important business is handled by the forty-two district courts. These are organised on a state basis throughout the republic.

At the lowest level petty cases are handled by a system of Justices of the Peace, with summary powers to fine and imprison. The procedure of the courts follows the usual pattern of Roman Law countries, with the judge conducting the case and directing enquiries before proceeding to trial. The general structure of the law is based on detailed written codes amplifying the general legislation of the country, and these codes are devised so as to allow minimal opportunity for variation.

Given the strong powers of the Mexican executive there would naturally be considerable concern in such a system as to whether the guarantees of personal liberties of the first twenty-nine articles of the Mexican constitution would in fact be effective. However, Mexican law contains a powerful provision known as the writ of Amparo, a legal device which combines the effectiveness of the English writ with the right of habeas corpus. The purpose of this writ is to restrain the federal government from actions damaging to the individual; anyone can apply for the writ for a federal court, which alone has the power to issue it, provided he has a case which is based securely on one of the provisions which enable it to operate. Such provisions include the rights to free petition and assembly, equality before the law, the right to travel and the right to work. The use of the writ does not form a precedent to future legal action, it merely restrains the application of the law in the particular case in which an appeal is granted, but its use has, in the past, often been recognised by government as a hint that the law ought to be changed.

THE STATES

The states are administered by a governor elected for a period of six years, but not necessarily at the same time as the president, and a single-chamber state legislature. Governors are chosen from among loyal supporters of the ruling party, and many of them are either lawyers or soldiers. A useful prelude to a governorship is frequently the holding of a seat as a federal deputy or in some cases a federal senator. The pronounced localism of Mexican politics, however, gives rise to a considerable degree of family interests in the states, and until 1940 many of the states were virtually controlled by their local political leaders. Since then, however, the network of interest has been broadened and although there is evidently a degree of continuity with the past, family interests cannot operate entirely unchecked nowadays. At the same time the struggles that occurred in the past between representatives of the local interests desiring independence and the power of the federal government is now checked by the operation of the interconnected network of the ruling party. Here, however, the governors are at a considerable advantage as against the state legislators in that they enjoy the all-powerful privilege of direct access to the president, and in so many issues involving federal expenditure and the control of federal funds it is the central government that has the last word.

The states themselves owe their very existence and their boundaries to this interplay between central and regional governments. Some of them, such as Oaxaca or Michoacán, represent the areas of pre-Hispanic tribes; others, such as Aguascalientes, represent early Spanish territorial divisions of government. However many others, such as the state of

Morelos, significantly named after the hero of Mexican independence, are artificial creations preserving the political dominance of a single statesman of the past. Today there are thirty-one states. Two were, until 9 October 1974, federal territories which were ruled directly by the federal government. These were the territories of Baja California del Sur in the north and Quintana Roo in the Yucatán peninsula. The Federal District is still ruled by a governor appointed by the incumbent president, and normally a very close associate of his.

THE MUNICIPALITIES

The states are divided for local government purposes into 2,365 municipalities. In the Federal District the equivalent unit is known as a delegation—there are eleven of these. The Mexican municipality, however, is not necessarily an urban area, for the entire country is divided into units of roughly equivalent population. The rapid growth of the Mexican population, however, and the pronounced drift from the provinces to the capital, have resulted in a wide disparity between the municipalities, but even the weakest of them is of political significance in that this area is the one that is closest to the support of the people. Nevertheless, some of them are extremely large and sparsely populated, particularly in the rural north, and a number of them have under 500 families. Many of these people live practically in the style of colonial times, but with some modern advantages such as bus transport, electricity and the products of mass production—even in the most remote hamlet the ubiquitous Coca Cola sign stands out.

Municipalities are administered by an elected official corresponding to a mayor, assisted by a small council.

THE CIVIL SERVICE

For the size of the country, Mexico enjoys a very large federal civil service, which is strongly centralised on the capital. Over 300,000 persons come within the scope of the principal civil service union, the FSTSE, which is a member of the popular sector of the PRI. In addition, there are in civil service employ some 55,000 teachers, who are separately organised.

The basic problem with the Mexican bureaucracy is that it has far too much to do. The Revolution has never succeeded in eradicating the petty corruption characteristic of pre-Revolutionary days—indeed, the post-war boom and the rapid growth of the economy, coupled with the increasing necessity to get hold of all kinds of permits and civil documents in order to earn a living, has resulted in the ubiquitous Mexican institution known as the *mordida* (literally 'bite'). Outright bribery is rare, and at higher levels at least, virtually unknown. But the easing of bureaucratic channels by the giving of small considerations is very frequent, and a recognised part of the Mexican way of life for Mexicans themselves. It should be emphasised that it is not a practice in which a foreigner is advised to engage on his own account. The present government of President Echeverría has announced a major crack down on corruption, and penalties are, at least potentially, heavy.

CURRENCY AND TAXATION

The basic unit of Mexican currency is the peso, which is divided into 100 centavos. The peso is the descendant of the ancient Spanish 'piece of eight', and is an enormous coin of the size of an American silver dollar or an English crown piece. Alas, it is made of a silver, copper and nickel alloy, as are smaller pieces of 50 and 25 centavos. Since 1951 the peso has been pegged to an exchange rate against the United States dollar of 12½ to 1 US dollar. It is therefore worth 8 cents in American money. Bronze coins of 50, 20, 10, 5 and 1 centavos, also circulate as do nickel coins of 10 centavos. Of these coins the most important is the peso itself, and the small 20 centavo piece or 'tostón', commonly used when tips are given. Notes start at 1 peso and go upwards in denominations of 5, 10, 20, 50, 100, 500 and 1,000 pesos. An awkward by-product of the small value of the Mexican peso is that a pocketful of Mexican change is extremely heavy, and, due to the weight of the currency, the development of automatic machines in Mexico, which would otherwise be expected in view of the country's proximity to the United States, has been considerably hampered.

The bulk of the federal revenue is raised from income tax (30 per cent) and taxes on industry and trade (approx 25 per cent). Taxes on imports and exports together account for approximately another 20 per cent. Surprisingly enough, in view of the heavy involvement in their economy, revenue from public services and natural resources account for only 7 per cent of federal revenue. This is a sum only slightly exceeding that raised by internal loans. The government operates an extensive system of tax exemptions to encourage business involvement in the rural areas and as industry has grown, so the burden of taxation has been transferred in their direction. Nevertheless, the taxation system as a whole is basically a conventional one, and it does not come as a surprise to discover that it stems from that developed in the 1920s when the introduction of income tax enabled the government to supersede the old dependence upon federal customs duties.

The federal income tax was completely revised by the Income Tax Law of 1965, and has since been amended annually. It is levied not only on individuals, but also on corporations, with the exception of government organisations and certain educational, charitable and non-profit associations. Before 1965 different categories of income were treated differently for tax purposes; since then they are considered together, although there are some differences in practice, income on investments, for example, being usually taxed at source while fees may only partly be so.

Income from personal services (which includes salaries, wages, professional fees, bonuses and employee's statutory participation in the profits of his employer), after a standard deduction of 20 per cent on the first 150,000 pesos, is taxed on a scale ranging from just below 4 per cent to 42 per cent, which is the top rate for an income of over 1·5 million pesos. However, income over 100,000 pesos per year is, after personal exclusions for the taxpayer, his wife and dependants and exclusions for permitted deductions (including medical and dental expenses, premiums on insurance policies, and certain expenses necessary to his occupation), subject to a tax on accumulated gross income which ranges from 13 to 42 per cent.

The taxation of income from capital, which is combined with that from personal services for the calculation of the accumulated gross income tax, is itself handled in a number of different ways, depending on the nature of the capital investment. Capital gains are taxed if gained from the sale within ten years of purchase of urban real estate other than the taxpayer's own residence, or on the sale of all securities not obtained on a Mexican stock exchange. Interest and miscellaneous capital income are taxed on a sliding scale ranging from 4 to 42 per cent, but dividends from investments are charged at a lower rate, subject to certain exceptions.

All taxpayers have to submit an income tax return in April of each year, and must pay the balance, if any, of unpaid taxes or claim back any excess paid at that time, or within three months. If he has paid too much the taxpayer will normally be given a credit against future taxes. If he has paid too little, and voluntarily pays the balance late, he may be surcharged, and if he is made to pay the balance involuntarily he may have to pay up to three times the tax assessed. All taxpayers are required to keep their returns and relevant documents for a period of five years after the filing of the return, and by law cannot be required to pay additional taxes relating to a period more than five years before.

Although capital gains are taxable in themselves and are also taxable under the federal accumulated gross income-tax system, there is no federal tax on inheritance. A few of the states levy inheritance taxes but the rates are low.

Apart from income tax, the only other important charge on the salary or wage-earner's pay packet is his contribution of 25 per cent of the cost of the social security provisions. This is withheld by the employer and transmitted to the government together with his own 62.5 per cent share. The balance is paid by the federal government itself out of general revenue. But this does not in any way exhaust the individual's liability to tax.

Indirectly he pays the cost of a great many different taxes on industry and trade. A general tax on gross receipts covers most forms of sales, rentals and leases and income from services of all kinds. Excepted are small businesses, particularly if they are in the food trade or certain occupations relating directly to economic development, but all sales on credit are taxable on the full amount of the sale. Generally included in the overall charge of 3 per cent is a 40 per cent share for the state or territory in which the transaction takes place; the federal government, in effect, acting as a tax-collection agency for the state concerned. Additional taxes are levied on luxury goods: 7 per cent on electronic articles—records, tapes, vacuum cleaners and floor polishers; 10 per cent on rugs, carpets and wall hangings unless made by hand in Mexico and containing a specified proportion of local fibres. Excise taxes are levied on alcoholic beverages, mineral waters, tobacco, and sugar, on the manufacture and use of motor-cars and lorries, on the use of the telephone services, and on a number of primary productive industries, including mining, cement, electricity and forestry.

How the Country Is Run

The states and municipalities use a wide range of taxes, the most important of which are those on income from capital, the gross receipts tax and a number of charges on the transfer and use of real estate. They are also responsible for the registration of motor vehicles, taxes on the sales of alcoholic beverages, and entertainments tax. These taxes are adequate for the purposes of the richer municipalities, but in general the revenue of the states is inadequate to make them truly independent of the federal government.

In assessing the impact of taxation two points may be helpful. Figures for all employed Mexicans are not available, but the average wage in the manufacturing industry in Mexico in 1970 was estimated at 1,677 pesos (£56 or $130) per month, which is just over 20,000 pesos per year. A wage earner entitled to a deduction of 9,000 pesos for himself, 6,000 for his wife, and 3,000 for each dependant child or parent pays very little income tax, if any, on this basic amount.

Secondly, there is an important provision of Mexican law that all businesses must distribute to their employees, excluding directors and senior executives, a proportion of their profits, usually about 12 per cent of their net income after tax. In addition, employees are entitled to the reversion of the employer's compulsory contributions to the National Workers' Housing Fund if they have not otherwise made use of them.

THE ECONOMY

The Mexican Revolution, for the inhabitants of the country, means spectacular economic growth, and growth that has been both steady and remarkably constant for many years now. As other countries have found, however, such growth imposes considerable strains on a society, which a government has to be prepared to meet and to ameliorate. The Mexican government seeks to do this in three main ways:

by protection of the economic rights of labour generally, by regional development, and by direct investment.

Regional development aims to spread the benefits of economic growth, and in particular to attempt to relieve the considerable strain on the region around the capital, which hitherto has been the magnet for every Mexican. Efforts to this end began in the early 1950s with the setting up of regional development organisations modelled on the Tennessee Valley Authority in the United States. Like TVA they were centred on river basins, partly for the reason that the hydro-electric potential of the basins offered the best chance for the growth of new industries, partly because no serious growth could be possible anywhere without regular and ample supplies of water.

Tax exemptions and other inducements have been given to encourage industries to move to these and to other development areas, and the federal structure offers the possibility of competition between the states in the inducements they offer. However, it remains a problem that the most important development in Mexico outside the immediate vicinity of the capital, with the special exception of Lower California, has been, not in new untapped areas, but in well-established regional centres like Puebla. The rural areas, therefore, have been most successfully helped by direct investment on a much smaller scale.

The government's investment is handled by a number of official bodies, but far and away the most important is Nacional Financiera, SA (Nafinsa). Originally created as a small finance company by President Rodríguez in 1933 for the purposes of carrying out limited rural development, it became in 1940 a major organ in the regulation of the securities market and the development of industrial enterprises. However, its primary purpose is not to invest in public securities, but in those of private Mexican enterprises through which the government exercises a considerable amount of indirect control on the development of the economy. The overwhelming proportion of Nacional Financiera's operations have practically been directed towards the development of transportation and communications, and in the expansion of the electrical-power industry. Together these account for over 50 per cent of its total investment, the balance being divided between basic industries such as oil, steel and cement, and manufacturing industries such as motor vehicles, paper, textiles, chemicals and food products.

Since 1940 the Mexican economy has grown at an astonishing rate, on average at 6 per cent per year, although at the same time the population has been rising at the rate of 3 per cent per year, so despite the fact that growth has meant substantial improvement in the lot of most Mexicans, a degree of imbalance has not only been retained but has in some cases actually been increased. Put in perspective, the government's success in achieving this degree of growth without much more rapid inflation must be compared with the performance of other Latin American countries such as Brazil and Argentina, where inflation rates have not only wholly eroded the gains of industrial development, they have actually resulted in a real loss. The dilemma presented by the conflict between the goal of economic growth and the social goals of the Revolution remains a very real one for Mexican politicians.

Abroad Mexico enjoys considerable respect on account of the strength of its economy, and there is no doubt that there would be many foreign enterprises very willing to invest there were it not for the well-justified suspicion with which the government regards any move towards domination of its economy by outside interests. All foreign enterprises, and foreign investment in Mexican enterprises, are subject to extensive limitations and restrictions; they pay higher taxes, and under the policy of 'Mexicanisation' are required increasingly (and, ultimately, totally) to be complementary and subordinate to domestic investment. A particular problem here has been that for many years there simply have not been sufficient resources in the private sector to provide private capital from the Mexican side for foreign businesses wishing to trade in Mexico. In effect, therefore, if they wish to do so they must enter partnership with the federal government, an unequal relationship which on entering they are required to declare they will not seek to counterbalance by calling on the aid of their own government (the so-called 'Calvo clause').

Mexicanisation, however, has been applied neither to enterprises established on the northern border, nor where articles cannot be produced in Mexico or the establishment of their production would result in the introduction of a new technology or otherwise benefit the Mexican economy, eg by export. Nor is there any control on the repatriation of foreign capital.

It is the continuing need to import manufactured goods that results in Mexico having a continuing, and in fact worsening, deficit on current balance of payments. This is not critical, since on account of its mineral wealth and because of the boom in tourist trade and for other reasons, Mexico has very substantial reserves of gold, silver and foreign exchange. The deficit was exacerbated by the bad harvest of 1970 to US $866 million; in 1971 it was reduced again to US $735 million, but since then has been rising. Some cause for concern has, however, arisen as a result of the increase in Mexico's foreign debt caused by the country's insatiable demand for capital to finance the government industrialisation programme. In 1960 debt service accounted for 16·2 per cent of foreign exchange earnings. By 1970 the proportion had risen to 23·5 per cent, service on the debt amounting to US $557 million in that year alone. Since 1971 the volume of new borrowings from abroad has been reduced in an effort to arrest this trend.

THE ARMED FORCES

The Mexican army derives from the 'Army of the Three Guarantees' formed to fight for Mexican independence in

1821, and ultimately from the colonial militia first formed during the Seven Years War to defend the Spanish colonies in the Indies from British attack. It does not do so directly, however. The old Federal army was utterly defeated by the Constitutionalist forces in 1914. Those forces, which were led and trained by a few men who had served under the old regime but the majority of whom learned their skills themselves on active service, became Mexico's present-day army when in the 1920s and 1930s it was given modern arms, professional training, and a new command structure.

Mexico, which was perforce neutral during World War I, entered World War II in 1942 when one of her tankers, the *Faja de Oro*, was torpedoed at sea by a German submarine with the loss of all her crew. A Mexican air squadron, Squadron 201, participated actively in the Pacific theatre.

Since 1945 the army has been continually modernised and is now a very up-to-date fighting force. It has 50 battalions of infantry, 2 infantry brigades, 21 cavalry regiments, 1 mechanised cavalry regiment, 2 artillery regiments and 2 coastal batteries, and is organised on the basis of 35 zones covering the entire country. Regular army establishment is 51,000 officers and men. Officers are trained in Mexico, in particular at the Escuela Nacional Militar, but some go for courses to the United States and other countries. Armament and uniform is in the American style. Command of the army is vested by the Constitution in the president himself, but is made effective through the secretaryship of defence, which also controls the air force.

At first sight it might seem curious that Mexico, with its long coastline and history of invasion maintains only a small navy. There are certainly historical reasons for this; neither the Maya nor the inland nations of Mexico seem to have developed large craft before the arrival of the Spaniards, and they in turn kept the control of the fleet, on which their supremacy depended, very much in their own hands by prohibiting the colonists from constructing vessels that could compete. Lack of an adequate navy was one of the reasons why the Spaniards were able to hold on to the island fortress of San Juan de Ulua in the bay of Veracruz until 1825, when they were expelled with the aid of British ships. Again, the French took the fortress with six ships in 1838, and it formed no barrier to the landing of the Americans in 1847.

Despite this, until the twentieth century the navy was very much neglected, although encouragement was given to maritime transport and the navy itself played an important role in preventing the secession of Yucatán. However, since 1938, when the nationalisation of Mexican oil compelled the government to invest in tankers and to protect them in time of war, a small but efficient coastal patrol service has been built up. It has 2 destroyers, 10 frigates, 15 escort minesweepers, and ancillary craft. Its establishment of some 11,000 men includes the equivalent of two regiments of marines.

The first ships built in Mexico were launched as early as 1628, but it appears that Mexican initiative and enterprise was not limited to the seas, for the first report of a Mexican attempting the conquest of the air dates from 1667. Unfortunately, neither his name nor the means which he employed was recorded. The first Mexican actually to make an aerial voyage was José María Alfaro, who flew in a free balloon of the Montgolfière type near Jalapa, now in the state of Veracruz, on 18 May 1784. A number of experiments with gliders were made towards the end of the nineteenth century. In 1872 one Carlos Antonio Obregón launched himself from one of the towers of the cathedral in Mexico City and, it appears, survived the experience. When powered flight was eventually achieved, several Mexicans rushed to emulate it, the first actually to fly being Alberto Braniff, who made the first flight in Mexico on 8 January 1910 on the site of what later became the Balbuena military airfield.

Military necessity then provided a powerful spur to further development. In April 1914 the Mexican air force became the first ever to take part in an aerial engagement, rather than simply engage in reconnaissance duties, when Constitutionalist aircraft bombed Federal ships off the coast of Mazatlán. By 1920, when regular civilian aviation began in Mexico, military aviation was well developed. It was to prove its worth in the abortive revolt of 1929, when 'spotter' aircraft laid bare the northern deserts (formerly the seat of insurgency) to government forces. The sudden ending of the last military revolt, that of 1938, merely emphasised the lesson. Today the air force has 5,000 men in its complement, with 160 aircraft, mostly training and transport machines, with an additional helicopter force. Like other Latin American air forces it comes under the United States' self-denying ordinance of excluding jet aircraft (other than trainers) from the Western hemisphere.

THE POLICE

Police organisation in the city of Mexico began with the creation by Congress in 1825 of the so-called *Celadores públicos*. The city police came directly under the administration of the municipal authority until 1896 when it was transferred to the control of the federal government. It has continued to be under federal government control, acting through the administration of the Federal District, ever since.

Outside the capital there was no general police organisation until the administration of Díaz. It was Díaz who recruited the rural police or *Rurales*, mainly from the numerous bandits who roamed the country in the early 1870s. On the principle that 'poachers make the best gamekeepers' the bandits were thus brought under military discipline, given handsome grey uniforms and broad sombreros, and armed to the teeth with the latest weapons. They were organised on the continental model, namely as a sort of *gendarmerie*, and as such were given a military education, subject to military discipline and expected to act in case of national emergency as a corps of the regular army. Control of the *Rurales* under normal conditions came under the *Jefe Político*, the chief political officer for a district comprising several municipalities, and so unconditionally loyal to the central government. Their well-deserved reputation for efficiency was much enhanced by the extensive powers they were given—for example, they had authority to shoot on the spot any person robbing a train.

After the revolution the *Rurales*, like the Federal army, were displaced by a Constitutionalist police force. This is the ancestor of the present police organisation which, outside the capital, comes directly under the control of the secretary of interior. Despite the European style of administration, training and uniforms are now very North American in style.

NATIONAL SYMBOLS

The national coat of arms is an eagle standing upon a *nopal* (cactus) branch holding a wriggling serpent in its beak. Its origin derives from the legendary foundation of Tenochtitlan in 1325. The Aztecs, or Mexica, had, according to legend, been told to journey until they found an eagle holding a serpent in its beak, and at that point to found their new capital. In memory of the event they adopted the eagle as their symbol, and so it has continued down to the present time.

The national flag is a vertical tricolor of green, white and red with the national coat of arms in the centre. The three colours were adopted by Agustín de Iturbide in February 1821, when he proclaimed the Plan of Iguala. The white represented the Catholic religion, the green the insurgent movement, and the red those elements of the Spanish population who supported independence. Originally the three colours were displayed diagonally, but after the entry into Mexico of the triumphal Army of the Three Guarantees, it was decreed on 2 November 1821 that the national flag would be of the same colours, but displayed vertically and in the order of green, white and red. It was Iturbide, too, who ordered the Mexican eagle crowned, to be displayed on the white band; the crown was subsequently removed at his fall. There was, however, some variation in the attitude in which the eagle was displayed until 1916, when President Carranza ordered that in future it be displayed in profile.

The Mexican national anthem (*Himmo Nacional*) appeared much later. It was the product of a national competition ordered by President Santa Anna on 12 November 1853. The decision of the jury of three fell in favour of the words written by the Mexican poet Francisco González Bocanegra. A further competition was then held to obtain a suitable tune, and the result of this competition was decided in favour of a Spanish composer, Jaime Nuno. Nuno, who was of Catalan origin, had been nominated as director of a regimental band which had gone to Cuba, then still a Spanish colony. After two years there he resigned, and was invited by Santa Anna to go to Mexico. The complete national anthem was sung for the first time in the Theatre of Santa Anna on 15 September 1854. Nuno subsequently spent most of the rest of his life in the United States, where he taught music, but returned to Mexico on two further occasions, the last time in 1904 on the fiftieth anniversary of his composition. He died in 1908. González Bocanegra, who, like Nuno, was born in 1824, the year of the establishment of the republic, and had played an important role in the cultural life of the capital as well as gaining a considerable reputation for his love poems, died in 1861.

4

How They Live

HOUSING

THE form and nature of Mexican housing has traditional and sharp differences between town and country. These differences are being rapidly eroded by the appearance of modern building materials, but this, too, is wholly in the Mexican tradition to accept the best available and to make use of it.

Virtually all Mexican country-dwellers live in villages. The isolated farmhouse, common in Europe or the United States, is virtually unknown. The standard form of the house group is a group of three buildings, either separate or adjoining, consisting of a main living unit, a kitchen (often a lean-to to the main building) and a granary. It is a form that goes back to pre-Columbian times, and the fittings are also still largely pre-Columbian in form: the earth or stone hearth, the sleeping mat and the pottery utensils. The principal modern elements are the steel knife, metal cans for carrying water, and such modern innovations as the sewing machine or transistor radio.

Construction depends on the materials available. Where stone is available, and the householder can afford it, walls will be of rubble. In the *tierra caliente* the main structures are made of vertical poles interwoven with thin saplings or maize stalks in a form of wattle which is frequently daubed with mud and painted white to reflect the sun. Where bamboo is available it is commonly used. On the central plateau and in the north the traditional building material is adobe or mud brick, a material which is, incidentally, sufficiently resistant to water to be used elsewhere as well. Adobe is made, if necessary, by the householder himself, from local clay formed into blocks some 12in by 24in and set out to dry in the sun. It is an excellent insulator against the heat. Its colour varies with the colour of the local clay, from charcoal grey, through near white, to brown and even orange-red.

Nowadays concrete blocks are replacing adobe, and in the north the typical rural dwelling is a functional box of concrete blocks, roofed with corrugated iron in place of the traditional curved tiles, and having on its roof a huge concrete water tank. No doubt it is very practical, but it is not at all pretty. It is however considerably better than the tiny shacks of the poorest countryfolk made of all kinds of scrap materials in which beaten-out petrol cans predominate. Fringes of suburbs of this sort appear in places on the edge of the big cities, and are even improvised on vacant lots within them. The poorest dwellings may still have thatch of maize straw, as was traditional for the poorest houses in the country, but many adobe houses have flat roofs constructed of a double layer of tile or brick with mud between for insulation.

Granaries are usually separate from the main building, and vary in construction according to the kind of grain stored; corn on the cob being stored (appropriately) in light structures of cornstalks, while shelled corn is kept in granaries of clay with thatched roofs. Turkeys and chickens often occupy a corner of the dwelling house, but in better houses there will be a separate stone building for them. The best rural houses will also have, to complete their group, a separate stone bath house with a low entrance and dome-shaped roof, in which steam is produced by throwing water on heated stones. It is, however, more usual for several families to share a communal one.

The village itself consists of several house groups set around a central plaza where the weekly market is held, in front of the church. Other than the principal thoroughfare, roads are of cobbles or earth. Stores have open fronts on the streets and otherwise resemble dwelling houses. The chief example of really modern architecture is usually the school building; many of the churches have now fallen into disuse, although the villagers maintain their religious devotions in the villages at local shrines of the saints, and in their homes in front of their own small house shrine.

From a distance, the presence of a city, as in other countries, is nowadays most plainly evidenced by a first glimpse of high blocks of flats or offices. In particular the government's own rehousing schemes tend to take the universal form of great slab-sided buildings set in unkempt and extensive open spaces. In architectural quality they are, perhaps, rather above the average, but the total effect is nevertheless rather intimidating. They form the most drastic and obvious contrast to the unattractive shanty towns which they seek to replace. In an interesting and worthwhile experiment the government has also sought to tap the traditional self-help of the rural Mexicans in the urban setting, by providing in selected areas piles of free building materials for them to use.

Water is even more precious to Mexico than oil:

Oil refinery at Poza Rica, Veracruz.

Taking drinking water to the rapidly expanding eastern suburbs of Mexico City.

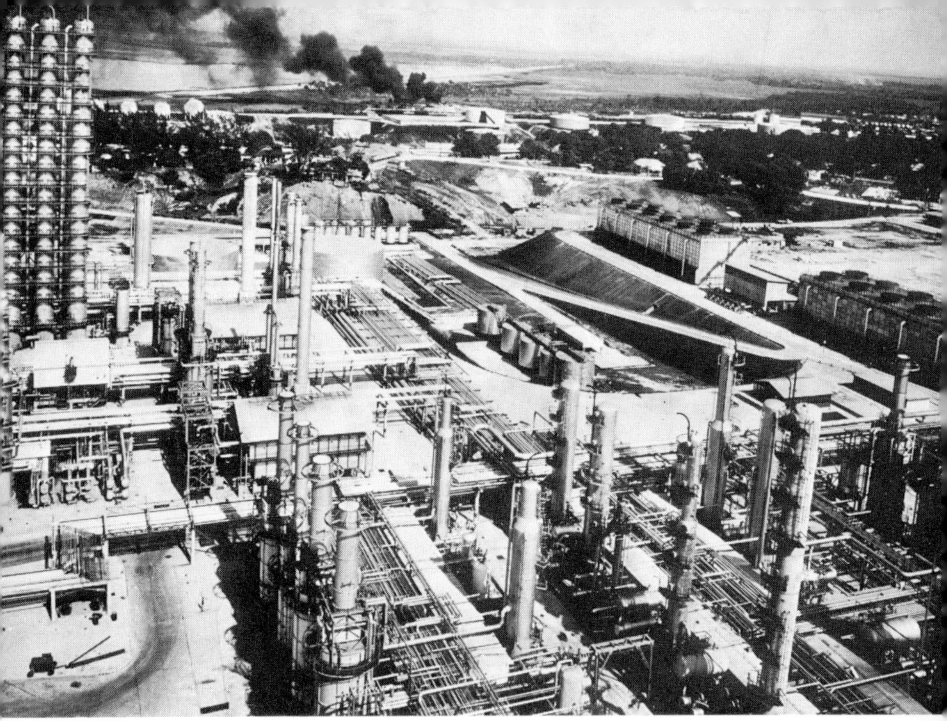

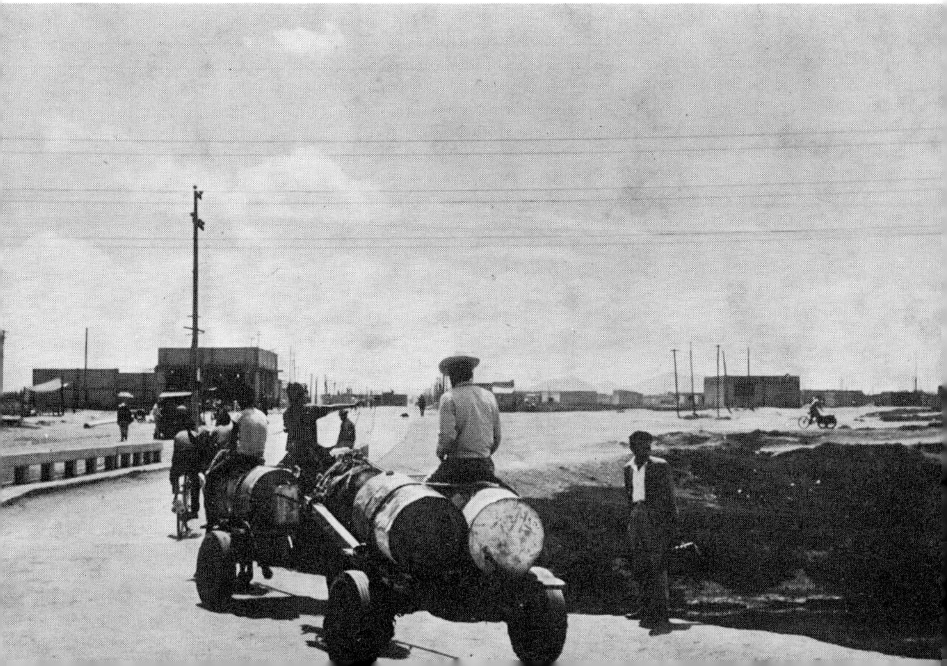

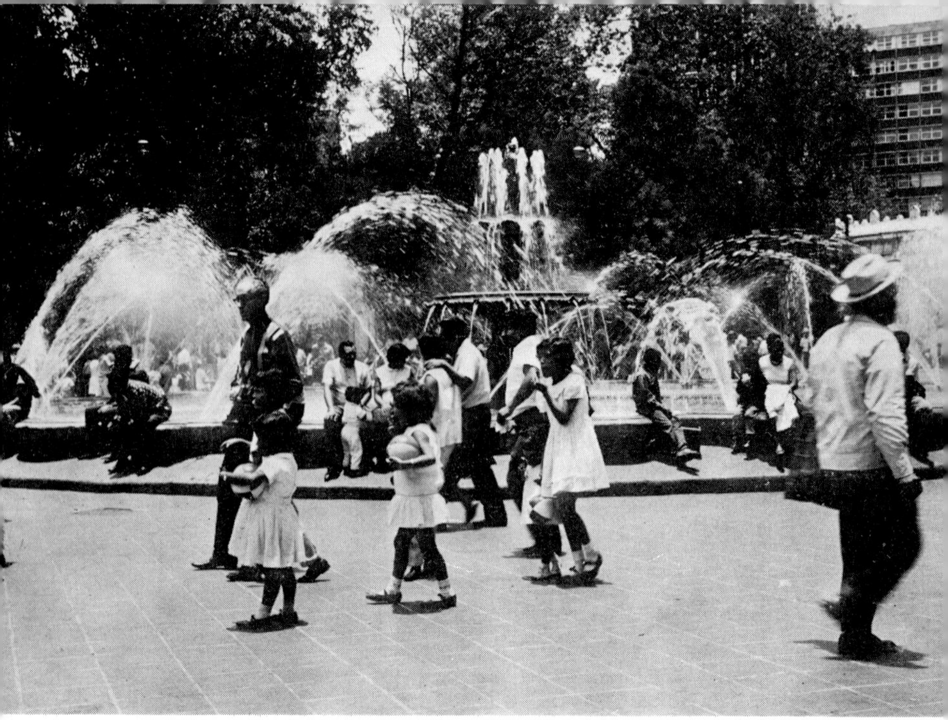

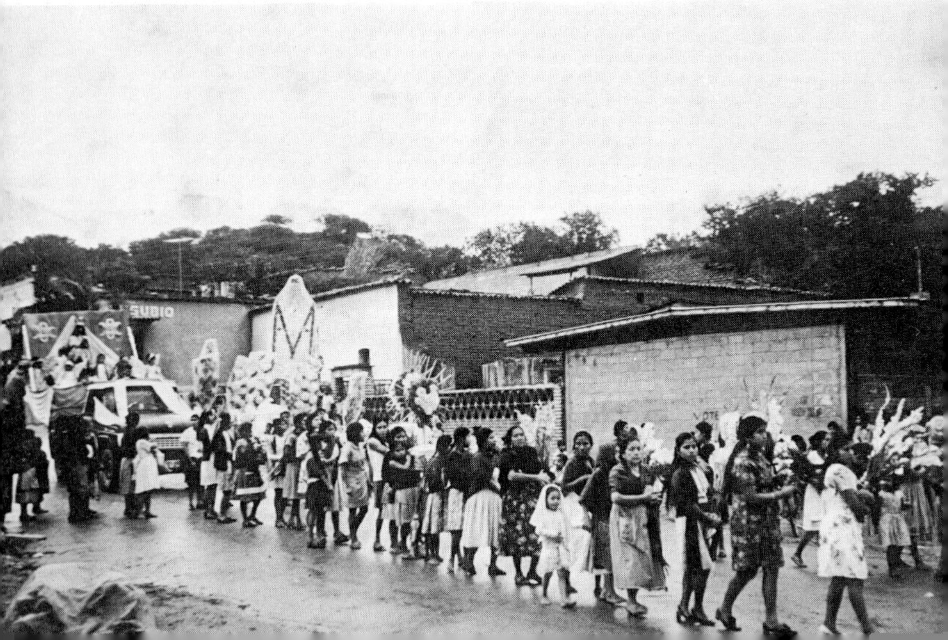
SUBIO

Traditional urban housing otherwise falls into three main categories, of which the dominant form is the courtyard house built round a patio. This is a defensive form which has permanently affected the design of cities and towns. From the outside the first impression is of few windows and a massive entrance door. The windows are barred with iron and the door, which is usually open during the day, opens into a short corridor leading into a colonnaded courtyard. There is, however, an inner gate which is kept closed. The courtyard is generally surrounded by rooms on all four sides, but in simpler houses two sides of the courtyard may be made up of blank walls. In recent years the courtyard may well have been roofed in and is in any case used as a communal eating area. In larger ones the servants' quarters are grouped around a secondary patio together with the domestic offices, and in the biggest two storeys may be employed with a balcony running round the courtyard at an upper level. Although in the capital itself houses in colonial as well as modern times did run to three storeys, the Palace of Iturbide in Mexico City is unique in having four, and was at the time of its building regarded with considerable astonishment and apprehension.

Religion remains of fundamental importance:

A Mexican family takes a Sunday walk in the Alameda, Mexico City.

A village procession of the Saints, State of Oaxaca.

The less well-to-do, if they are able to afford reasonable housing, live in single buildings, square and regular, like their rural equivalents. At the other end of the scale there are in most large Mexican cities wealthy, and often extremely wealthy, residential suburbs laid out in a fashion which permits the attainment of heights of luxury almost undreamed of by the poor. American influence often predominates in the design of ranch-style dwellings today, but the Hispanic influence is still strong, and characteristic interior fitments will include the familiar blue tiles of Puebla, the use of Mexican mosaic to decorate walls, and the multitude of local silver and onyx ornaments. Very affluent Mexicans often live in isolated suburbs for the protection of which they contribute to the maintenance of a common private security organisation. Of such suburbs, that built on the lava flow of the Pedregal, on the outskirts of Mexico City, is the wealthiest and the most famous.

In Mexican urban centres, which in the last century were often influenced by French elegance in the shape of ornamental street furniture and the ubiquitous bandstands, the modern distinguishing feature is the presence at irregular intervals of buildings on drastically different scales. Some of these will be hotels, others the offices of large corporations; in the capital itself, and in certain of the other large cities, they occur in sufficient quantity to form an entirely new dimension of town planning.

The unsatisfactory state of much of the housing of Mexico would undoubtedly be infinitely worse were it not for the relatively benign nature of the climate. Nevertheless, the social strains which it indicates have led to considerable political problems, and no Mexican government can afford to be complacent about the disparities in wealth which the nature of its housing evidences. A major problem is the dominant pattern of the drift of the population towards the Core, combined with the very rapid natural increase in population in that area.

The upshot was that the 1970 census disclosed that the

48 million population was living in only 8,286,000 households, with an average of 5.8 persons per household. Two-thirds were owner occupiers. These figures, however, tell only part of the story and the true dimensions of the problem can only be gauged from the information that these households averaged only 2.3 rooms each, with 2.5 persons per room. Forty per cent of all dwellings, in fact, consisted of only one room.

Overcrowding also places a particular strain on ancillary facilities, especially around Mexico City itself. Water is one problem. Only 38 per cent of all Mexican households enjoy piped water supply, and in many of the outlying suburbs twenty or more families may have to share a single communal tap. Drainage is an even worse problem. Although 41.5 per cent of Mexican homes have a toilet of some kind, far fewer have flush toilets and at present in the poorer parts one simple soakpit may serve the needs of the entire community. Around the capital it is the difficulty of providing mains drainage that has limited the growth of new suburbs. Electricity seems to be less of a problem. Official returns show that 58.9 per cent of Mexican homes have electric lighting, and there is reason to believe that with considerable ingenuity others have been illuminated by illegally tapping public sources. In the country districts kerosene lanterns continue to be the rule.

On 1 May 1972 the government of President Echeverría inaugurated a new programme designed to grapple with the problem of urban housing by setting up the Instituto Nacional del Fondo para la Vivienda de los Trabajadores (INFONAVIT), a federal agency made up of the representatives of the government, the employers and labour, charged with administering the Fondo Nacional de la Vivienda (FONAVI) or National Workers' Housing Fund. Employers are required to contribute the equivalent of 5 per cent of the ordinary salary of their employees to this fund, from which in turn the workers can borrow for buying, extending or making improvements to their housing. If they do not do so, the savings are held in trust for them and can be withdrawn on retirement or paid on decease to the worker's heirs. It is, in effect, a government-sponsored building society. Incidentally, employers are also required to contribute the equivalent of 1 per cent of their employees' salaries to a separate fund for the maintenance of education.

FOOD AND DRINK

The Mexicans have, not just cookery, but a cuisine. Their system of eating still rests on its pre-Conquest foundations of maize, black beans and squash, enlivened with chillies. The indigenous turkey has been displaced almost entirely by the cheaper chicken, and of course modern Mexicans enjoy a possibility of eating a wide range of European and American style foods, including the ubiquitous convenience foods in tinned, preserved or frozen form.

The basis of Mexican cooking is the tortilla. A tortilla is a round pancake of unleavened maize, which forms not only the Mexican staple bread, but for the poorer members of the community serves also as a plate and as a napkin for wiping the mouth after eating. Tortillas are made by first soaking maize in lime water, after which it is parboiled. It is then ground into a paste in a stone implement known as the *metate*—in modern bakeries this will be done by machine—and the paste is then shaped into a ball and patted out into its pancake form by being tossed from hand to hand in the air. The characteristic noise of tortillas being beaten out by hand can be heard in every town in the country at appropriate times of day. Once made, the tortillas are cooked on a flat griddle, over a charcoal fire traditionally, until they are pale golden brown in colour. A stack of them will accompany any properly served Mexican meal, preferably wrapped up in a napkin in a small basket.

A wide range of dishes are derived directly from the tortilla by simply putting something in it and rolling it up.

This filling may be anything from simple chopped onion to a bean or meat stew. Tortillas filled with beans, highly seasoned and served with chilli sauce are known as *enchiliadas*, and are one of the basic standbys of Mexican cooking. Alternatively, the tortilla, once baked, may be filled and then fried, a dish which is known as a *taco*. These and similar dishes, however, do not form a complete meal; they are served with a wide range of accompaniments, of which the most celebrated is an innocent-looking pale green cream of avocado. When tasted by the unwary, these and similar Mexican delicacies turn out to be very highly seasoned indeed, and any Mexican meal is at least potentially full of exciting surprises. Mexicans like their food extremely hot, and at its strongest Mexican cooking compares with the best in Indian cooking for the ferocity of its condiments and the amount of application needed to eat it.

The most celebrated of all Mexican dishes is turkey with *mole* sauce. The turkey is cooked slowly in the sauce, the basic ingredient of which is dark bitter chocolate, itself a Mexican product, and one which still bears almost unaltered its Aztec name. There are some twenty-three other ingredients also, including onions, garlic, almonds, chilli and tomatoes. The preparation of *mole*, which is served in most Mexican families on special feast days, is a great art involving a very long period of cooking and preparation beforehand, and the art of making it is one which is carefully transmitted from mother to daughter.

Like Spaniards Mexicans rise early, before it gets hot. Many of them have no more breakfast than a cup of black coffee, sweetened with caramelised sugar. However, many Mexicans will eat some reheated beans wrapped in a tortilla, and another popular breakfast dish is fried eggs with chilli sauce. The main meal of the day is served between 2 and 3 pm—later at weekends—and consists of a number of courses accompanied by beans or rice and various sorts of sauce and salad. The Mexicans do not eat their evening meal as late as the Spaniards—between 7 and 8 is the usual time. The menu for this is very similar to that of the main meal of the day (*comida*), but in addition a sweet pastry or similar lighter delicacies are often served.

Between meals all classes of Mexicans enjoy numerous soft drinks which are sold from stores in the markets and on street corners everywhere. Papaya juice, lime and water melon are the traditional refreshing drinks for a warm climate, but there are now numerous bottled products to compete with them, including of course the inevitable Coca-Cola. Because of the scarcity of safe drinking water, bottled mineral water is also enjoyed and has a wide sale. Bottled beer from the huge Moctezuma Brewery in Monterrey is also a familiar sight. Any or all of these may accompany a meal, although Mexicans of the wealthier classes also drink wine, some of which is actually produced in Mexico but is not very highly regarded by the Mexicans.

The indigenous alcoholic drinks are pulque and tequila. Pulque is distilled from the freshly tapped juice of the maguey cactus. When fermented it becomes a clear, somewhat cloudy liquid with a distinctive odour, and it has a considerable alcoholic content. Tequila, a derivative distilled from it, is a clear and apparently harmless-looking liquid but it has a very high alcoholic content indeed. Mexican style, it is drunk by the tot at a single gulp and then followed by salt, fresh lime and tomato juice in an almost ritualistic sequence. The effects, which are startling, have to be felt to be believed.

PRIVATE CONSUMPTION

Foodstuffs account for by far the highest proportion of the budget of the average Mexican (who consumes 2,620 calories a day including 62g of protein). Next comes housing and its ancillary services, in particular the supply of drinking water and electricity.

Clothing gives the sharpest indicator of differences between urban and rural Mexico. In 1960 14 per cent of the

Mexican population still went barefoot and a further 23 per cent regularly wore sandals rather than shoes. Sandals, traditionally made of vegetable fibres but in modern times often soled with cut-down motor-car tyres, are, in fact, the traditional rural footgear for Mexico just as the familiar white pyjama-like garments and large hat are the traditional rural clothing. However, the opening up of the country, particularly by means of the bus, means that a widely contrasting range of products are available in the local stores as well as in the cities; and in many cases many rural Mexicans may now travel easily to and from market to exchange the produce of their fields for modern cosmetics, modern clothes and such signs of newly acquired status as a transistor radio.

At the same time, certain important economic elements have entered the rural way of life which have enormously broadened its potentialities. In particular the sewing machine, the most widespread of the products of modern technology to be found in Mexican homes, offers the opportunity to women as well as men to contribute to the income of the home in a socially acceptable manner. This is a second reason why the visible change on Mexican consumption patterns represented by the diversification of clothing is perhaps the best indicator of social change in the countryside.

This is doubly important since that sector of the population which can contribute to the economy is, owing to the rapid rise in population, surprisingly small. No less than 46 per cent of all Mexicans are fifteen years of age or less. This proportion will remain approximately the same for the next decade or so, and may even increase. It is expected that the population will double between 1970 and 1990. Yet in 1970 only 14·8 million of a population of 48 million were classified as economically active, and of these at least half were farm labourers who work for no more than six months in the year. In fact, of the 14·8 million, the income of at least 10 million did not exceed the statutory minimum wage. Not only, as we shall see, does this create enormous problems for the financing of an adequate social-security system, it indirectly means that the domestic market for Mexican products is very small. Mexico, therefore, is necessarily a high-tariff nation in order to protect her local industries from competition, particularly from the United States and Japan.

In 1971 production of television sets of Mexican manufacture was 391,000, of refrigerators (something more than a luxury in a subtropical country) 212,000, and of motor-cars 153,398. These figures reflect the ability of the market to absorb the products which a keen and highly professional advertising industry encourage the urban population to buy. So, the output of consumer goods is primarily restricted by purchasing power, although it can safely be said that over the next decade or so, as one after another article becomes the next desirable purchase, the market will continue to expand and consumer durables become commonplace at least among the urban population.

An important social consequence of this limitation in an urban setting, as well as the general shortage of housing, is the general survival of domestic help in the home. Middle-class Mexicans still take such help for granted, and well-to-do families may employ a number of servants. Living conditions for these servants vary with the interest and concern of the family; at worst they and several of their dependants may be huddled in small shacks on the roof or in the back yard, at best they may have their own rooms and reasonable facilities. Domestic servants fell outside the scope of the social-security system before 1973 and so information is therefore difficult to come by. Furthermore, it is clearly a matter of status among middle-class Mexicans to have help in the home, regardless of whether or not their purchasing power is sufficient to replace it with a modern kitchen and all the labour-saving devices.

HEALTH

As a subtropical country, Mexico has in the past had to

contend with many serious kinds of illness, which in colonial and early modern times reached epidemic proportions. Typhoid, typhus, yellow fever, tuberculosis and the mysterious *cocolistle* (possibly influenza) were periodic and widespread scourges. The pre-Hispanic peoples had a considerable empirical medical knowledge, embodied in the Codex Badiano, a herbal remedy of 1552, translated from Náhuatl into Latin at the command of the then viceroy and now in the Vatican library. In addition they were aware of the principal functions of the human body and used fire to sterilise their medical instruments. Nor were the Spaniards backward at providing for their own health and that of their conquered people. Cortés himself founded several hospitals, one of which, the Hospital de la Concepción de Nuestra Señora in Mexico City (1521) is still in existence as a modern hospital. Others were added by the numerous religious orders and other benefactors. From its foundation, medicine was taught in the Royal University of Mexico, and has continued to be one of the most highly regarded professions.

Today Mexican medicine compares favourably with the best the world has to offer. Many of the country's medical staff are trained in the United States or have studied there for a time, so there is considerable interchange of ideas, and doctors are frequently fluent in English as well as in their own language. Unfortunately, such skilled medical care, coupled with the vast improvement in public health over the last fifty years, has given Mexico an immense problem with which to cope, in terms of one of the world's most rapidly growing populations. There were in 1968 some 33,981 doctors in Mexico, or one for every 1,445 persons, and 31,208 nurses, including midwives. As far as hospitals were concerned the situation was somewhat better, largely as a result of the immense efforts made by the government to cope with the situation in recent years. Mexico's 3,055 hospitals had in 1971 a total of 86,151 beds, or one bed for every 549 persons. Responsibility for the provision of many of these, as for the supervision of public health throughout the republic, is vested in the Department of Health and Assistance (SSA), founded in 1943.

Expectation of life is rising annually, and in 1970 the expectation of life at birth for a boy was 58·9 years and for a girl 63·1 years. By European standards (England and Wales, 1970: boy 68·8 years, girl 75·2 years) these figures are still on the low side, yet it must always be remembered that Mexico is not a European country and that although most of it may now generally be described as healthful, some parts still are not. This fact is reflected in the principal recorded causes of death. In 1970 a total of 485,656 deaths were recorded. Of these the principal group, 77,094, were caused by pneumonia or related illnesses; 69,410 by gastritis, enteritis etc; 65,304 from old age and other uncertain causes; and 25,222 from diseases of early infancy. Among the others the one that stands out most surprisingly is the figure for homicide, in which for many years Mexico has ranked top of the world league.

SOCIAL SECURITY

Social security was promised in the Constitution of 1917 as a basic right of every worker, and its basic principles spelt out in the Labour Code of 1931. However, its implementation was hampered by lack of financial resources, and so it was not until 1943 that the law was passed under which was established the principal agency of social security in Mexico, the Instituto Mexicano de Seguridad Social (IMSS). In contrast with the horizontal approach often used in other countries—that of supplying a limited service to all workers —Mexico has favoured instead a vertical approach, seeking to make available a full range of services to certain classes of workers, and extending these to other groups as resources allow.

Today the IMSS covers its beneficiaries against industrial accidents and professional ailments, maternity, non-industrial sickness, old age, retirement and death. Its beneficiaries are all those covered by a contract of work, in the public utilities, manufacturing industry, commerce, catering, transport and mining, throughout the republic. Workers in agriculture, including those members of the state co-operative farms (of whom more is said in the next chapter), and in forestry are also covered, but only in thirteen of the thirty-two governmental entities of the republic. In addition to the beneficiary himself, benefits are also payable to his wife or *compañera*, his children under the age of sixteen, and his parents and grandparents as applicable. In 1971 the service covered 10,501,241 people in all, representing approximately 20 per cent of the total population of the country, but the number covered has grown over the last ten years at a rate of over 12 per cent per year, and it is intended ultimately to extend benefits to all workers.

In addition to the benefits it offers in cash, the IMSS also offers a wide range of services. These include industrial-training schemes, labour exchanges, rural clinics, creches, youth clubs and sports centres. Most important, perhaps, is the integral medical service.

Workers in government departments and the public corporations, including employees of the Federal District and Federal Territories, are separately protected by the Instituto de Seguridad y Servicios Sociales para Trabajadores del Estado (ISSSTE), which was organised in 1960 on the basis of the former Directorate of Civil and Military Pensions. It offers to its members, who comprise approximately 4 per cent of the total population of the country, the same services as the IMSS, with the important addition of facilities for property and land credit, mortgages and short-term loans. Members of the armed forces, comprising 0·4 per cent of the total population, enjoy, together with their dependants, similar facilities from the Dirección General de Seguridad Social Militar (1962), which also finances land-resettlement schemes and fishery co-operatives for its members or beneficiaries.

Social security in Mexico is funded by a combination of contributions from worker and employer, together with assistance from the government. Its financial viability depends, significantly, on the relatively high membership of urban employees. Unemployment is not covered, and statistics for the rate of unemployment, as in many other countries and most in Latin America, are not available.

Care of the aged, as in other countries in which the extended family remains the basis of society, is still regarded by most Mexicans as being primarily a family duty. In this respect large families also act as a form of social insurance. Together with the care of the chronic sick, the gap between resources and need is filled by a number of voluntary organisations.

5
How They Work

By far the largest sector of the economically active population of Mexico is engaged in agriculture. Of these, the bulk is engaged primarily in subsistence farming—that is, in the production of the basic staples of the Mexican diet: corn, beans and chillies. In fact, less than 10 per cent of the land area of Mexico is suitable for arable cultivation. In terms of area, by far the greatest covered by an economically active population is that devoted to stockrearing, which will be considered separately. It amounts to approximately 35 per cent of the total land area. Forest accounts for 20 per cent, and forestry is a significant industry, if a relatively minor one in economic importance.

But it is upon its ability to produce food that the rapidly increasing population of Mexico primarily depends, and always has depended. Efficient agriculture for Mexico in the 1970s is not merely desirable economically, it is essential in human terms. The problem is that the attempt to make agriculture efficient runs in important respects directly contrary to the pattern of revolutionary change on the land. There always has been a basic conflict between the desire to increase production and the requirement that the land be distributed more equitably. In the 1920s, the distribution of land was slowed down while the government considered the problem that would arise if the subdivision of the land were to be carried as far as, for example, in contemporary France. In the 1930s the government of President Cárdenas found an alternative solution in the co-operative farm or *ejido* as it is known in Mexico.

The setting up of the *ejidos* in the 1930s was a mark not only of the radicalisation of the Mexican Revolution, but in the extent of commitment to the collective principle. In productive terms, however, its problem was that it reduced the sense of individual responsibility towards the land, while at the same time not by any means excluding the possibility of political control by influential local entrepreneurs. Postwar distributions of land, although generous in terms of area, have in some respects naturally made the situation worse, for the bulk of the land distributed since 1946 has necessarily consisted of relatively low-grade territory only capable of production with considerable financial aid. The difficulty with this is that apart from the government itself, the only people who can afford to do this are generally private companies; and many landholdings are too small: some 65 per cent being under 1 hectare (2·471 acres).

AGRICULTURE

From the outside, the most striking thing about Mexican agriculture is the extent to which it contributes to the country's exportable surplus. Mexico, still essentially a primary producer and an importer of manufactured goods, is dependent upon the export of agricultural products to a considerable extent in order to balance her international budget. Abroad, therefore, Mexico is seen as being one of the more influential of the world's producers of sugar, cotton and coffee. In fact, by far the most important part of Mexico's agricultural production is that dedicated to basic foodstuffs. Its production of maize runs at about 8·6 million tonnes annually, and is supplemented by a further production of over 2 million tonnes of wheat. Together with the indigenous crop of beans, chillies and squash, Mexico is, therefore, still able to feed its enormous population with its basic foodstuffs, but it is to some extent an importing nation in terms of luxuries; although it is a coffee producer, Mexico nevertheless continues to import a considerable amount of different types of coffee from other countries. It has been self-sufficient in terms of wheat since 1959, no mean task in a country in which the demand for this higher-priced product is a symbol of increasing wealth and status.

It would be misleading to leave the subject of Mexican agriculture without referring to one or two other products, for it is in the light of these that the country has so frequently been regarded. Mexico, which gave the world the tomato, today grows them in large quantities for export to the United States. It also produces 80 per cent of chicle, which forms the base of chewing gum. As befits the country which originated the name 'chocolate', Mexico is also still a substantial cocoa-producing nation, and most if not all of the cocoa locally consumed is grown in the country, although other countries are very much larger producers. Finally, as might be expected in a semi-tropical country with a considerable rainfall over low-lying areas, rice, since its introduction, has continued to grow well. Mexico has gone to great pains to increase its rice production over the past two decades and has done so with a considerable measure of success.

TABLE 2: AGRICULTURE (1969)

	'000 tonnes
Bananas	986
Beans	899
Coffee	165
Maize	8,600
Oranges	882
Rice	417
Sisal	160
Sugar cane	27,600
Tomatoes	581
Wheat	2,060

STOCKRAISING

Northern Mexico is still a great stockraising area, with something of the flavour of the old West. Some 37·7 million cattle and 6·7 million sheep roam this gigantic area. They are raised as in North America in gigantic ranches under the care of the traditional Mexican cowboy. The striking black costume affected by the Mexican cowboy on festival days, ornamented with braid and silver, has of course found considerable favour north of the Rio Bravo, and is familiar to everyone who has ever seen a 'western' movie. Horses are still extensively used, although for most carrying purposes Mexicans now rely on ancient and often very decrepit trucks.

The use of horses in arable cultivation is rapidly declining, and Mexico itself manufactures tractors. At the other end of the scale a great deal of cultivation in the small pocketed valleys of the south is still carried on largely by hand, perhaps with the aid of a donkey.

Pork forms an important item in the Mexican diet, and some 14·5 million pigs are kept all over the nation with a further 13·2 million goats supplying an alternative source of meat.

Strenuous efforts are being made to educate the people:

Public letter writers, Mexico City.

The Palace of Sport, Mexico City.

ESCRITORIO
PUBLICO
ESCRITORIO
CARMELO
ESCRITORIO
PUBLICO
FOTOSTATICAS
Escritorio PUBLICO
Chilian
TRASPASOS
DRENAJES
155A

S LOS MEXICANOS,
O UN SOLO HOMBRE,
UN SOLO HOMBRE:
ATRIOTA PRESIDENTE

TABLE 3: LIVESTOCK (1967)

	millions
Cattle	37·7
Donkeys	3·6
Goats	13·2
Horses	5·2
Mules	2·0
Pigs	14·5
Poultry	95·0
Sheep	6·7

FORESTRY

Mexico's timber lands extend over some 95 million acres and contain many of the finest woods used in commerce. Pine, spruce, cedar, mahogany, logwood and rosewood are all found in Mexico, and most of them are commercially exploited. Unfortunately, the casual attitude of the past to the conservation of natural resources, and the cutting down of many of the most accessible forests for charcoal burning, have resulted in severe depredations, in some places accom-

The ceremonial side of life is not forgotten—a presidential parade in Mexico City.

panied by widespread soil erosion and loss of fertility. Most serious of all has been the decline in water supplies. Rainwater is no longer held in the soil by the roots of the trees, and it runs away unchecked. Finally, in 1951 the Federal government stopped all timber cutting in twenty-two of the Mexican states, declaring null all existing concessions for timber exploitation.

Today the manufacture of wooden articles has been resumed, and important by-products include not only chicle but also pitch, turpentine and bark for tanning. Forest reserves cover some 1,977,000 acres (800,000 hectares), and there are forty-seven national park forests covering an almost equivalent area. The national parks, which are well run and supervised, constitute an important recreational area for masses of ordinary Mexican citizens who can now afford the motor transport to get there.

FISHING

Due to the dangerous nature of the coasts, the Mexican fishing industry has been very much on a small scale, and it was not until 1952, with the administration of President Ruiz Cortines, that in the celebrated 'drive for the sea' campaign a programme was initiated for developing coastal fishing in order to supply a valuable source of protein.

Shrimp fishing ranks first in importance, and a great deal of the catch is exported to the United States, where it commands a high price. Some 45,000 men are engaged in the coastal fishing industry. In addition, fishing is also carried out on the important inland lakes, and the famous butterfly nets of the fishermen on Lake Patzcuaro are familiar to tourists. In ancient times, the Aztecs must have relied heavily upon fishing to supply the population of their settlements in the Valley of Mexico, but with drying up and the pollution of the waters there this source has now practically disappeared.

SISAL

Sisal, or, as it is known in Mexico, *henequén*, is grown extensively in the plantations in the Yucatán peninsula. In the nineteenth century, conditions on these plantations were extremely backward, and the Maya inhabitants of Yucatán were heavily exploited by wealthy landowners, many of whom built themselves substantial homes on the outskirts of Mérida. The revolution in the state of Yucatán took the specific form of expropriating the plantations, and throughout the revolutionary years the state of Yucatán exercised direct control over the sale of sisal, which, unfortunately for them, was then undergoing a serious recession in world demand. The plantations themselves continued to be privately owned, but in 1955 they were grouped together into a single unified organisation in order to attempt to compete with the new artificial fibres which have largely displaced sisal on the world market in the manufacture of ropes, netting etc. Again, in 1964, this monopoly was taken over by the government, and is now administered by a state commission and employs some 250,000 workers. Mexico now produces approximately half of the world's supply. Unfortunately, this rate of production is too much for the market, which is unable to absorb it, and so the state of Yucatán has suffered serious economic recession in recent years, out of which it appears it is only just beginning to emerge.

IRON AND STEEL

Monterrey, the third largest city in Mexico, is the centre of the iron and steel industry, which in turn is second only in Latin America to that of the Volta Redonda in Brazil. This results from the fortunate coincidence that gives Mexico both extensive iron-ore reserves and coal of coking quality, although unfortunately for the Mexicans, they do not occur very close together. Iron ore is bought principally from the Cerro de Mercado in the state of Durango and from Golondrinas in the state of Nuevo León. The coal, on the other hand, comes from Sabinas in the state of Coahuila. Total annual production of iron and steel is around 2 million tons, and represents a very large proportion of Latin American output.

On this base, a large network of secondary industries has grown up around Monterrey, not only utilising steel itself but also producing consumer goods such as beer, cigarettes and glassware, while as an urban centre Monterrey has also naturally attracted the industries depending upon agricultural produce. Since 1960 steel production in Mexico has been in Mexican hands, and the state is behind a drive to open up an important new reserve of iron ore at Zihuatanejo on the coastline of Guerrero. The newer plants finish steel into a wide range of usable products, such as structural steel girders, tubes and pipes, wire nails and tinplate. In all these respects Mexico is now independent of foreign imports. The growth of steel production has also led to a dramatic expansion of the tinplate industry, and the use of sheet steel of heavier gauge has been expanded in the field of consumer goods. A problem of the Mexican steel industry is that since it is relatively modern, it employs a relatively small number of workers, not on the whole exceeding 20,000 men, but its contribution to the overall health of the Mexican economy is enormous.

GOLD AND SILVER

The Spaniards were attracted to Mexico in the first instance, of course, by the reports which they had received in the Caribbean islands of its legendary wealth in gold. Gold, which was not as highly regarded by the Aztecs as jade, was indeed worn extensively by them as ornament, but the resources of gold in Mexico itself turned out to be very much less than the Spaniards had hoped. It was through the mining of silver that Mexico contributed so overwhelmingly to the wealth of the Spanish empire, and to this day Mexico remains the world's largest silver-producing nation.

In colonial times gold was extracted by the amalgamation process. The mercury for this process came from Spain itself, and the monopoly which Spain had on it was a powerful factor in its control of the economy of the Indies. After independence, the lure of gold continued to draw hopeful outsiders to Mexico, and at the end of the rule of Díaz there were more than 300 companies formed to extract gold in Mexico. Few of them ever achieved much success, and a major problem for all of them, as for all mining in Mexico, lay in the very difficult terrain in which the mines lay. The shortage of water in the Sierra Madre was not only an inconvenience in the process of separation, it was even more critically a danger to the actual lives of the miners themselves. But the lure of gold notoriously overcomes all obstacles. Although small, the exports of gold from Mexico today are still a significant part of its national economy.

Silver, on the other hand, overwhelmingly dominates the Mexican mining scene. By the end of the nineteenth century it was estimated that at the time the total production of silver in Mexico must have exceeded some $4,000 million. These vast quantities were won by the most primitive methods. Shafts, often hundreds of feet deep, were worked with windlass and mule power, and in places even ladders were used for miners to reach the bottom of the shafts. The separation of silver was carried out by the patio process, which also made use of mercury. The crushed ore was amalgamated with mercury in the presence of copper nitrate and salt, the mixing being carried out by the use of mules. Stirring over a period of weeks resulted in the amalgamated silver falling to the bottom of the tank, and the silver was then separated from the mercury by the process of distillation—a process which, because of the intensely poisonous nature of mercury, claimed many miners' lives. The process was invented by Bartolomé Medina in 1557, and remained in use until the present century. Today it has been completely superseded by modern smelting methods.

Mexico's production of silver plays an important role in balancing its external trade. Some 16,000 oz are exported annually, and the production of silver articles and silver plate is an important industry, with a large market among visiting tourists.

OTHER MINERALS

Fortunately for Mexico, the mining industry covers a wide range of products besides gold and silver. Most important are the non-ferrous metals, in particular lead, zinc and copper. Copper production was already important in colonial times, and was responsible, indeed, for the development of large sections of northern Mexico. Today it is overshadowed by the much larger copper industries of other countries, but it still forms a significant proportion of total exports. Rising world prices for these humble but essential metals contributes considerably to the present health of the Mexican economy.

In addition, Mexico is fortunate in having substantial deposits of more exotic metals. Antimony, arsenic, cadmium, molybdenum, mercury and tungsten are all found and exploited, as is manganese, an essential ingredient in the making of stainless steel. The total number of workers employed in these industries is not large, but they are widely dispersed and form a significant element of the population of the northern areas.

One particularly interesting product of Mexican mining enterprise, although not a metal, must not be overlooked in this context. This is sulphur, which is obtained in a nearly pure state from the craters of Mexico's numerous extinct or dormant volcanoes. Sulphur, which together with saltpetre—also found in Mexico—forms the principal raw material of gunpowder, ironically played a major role in enabling Spain to conquer Mexico. Today, however, it fulfils a much-needed

TABLE 4: MINERALS (1971)

	tonnes
Antimony	3,361
Arsenic	8,717
Barytes	279,742
Bismuth	570
Cadmium	1,662
Cement	7,521,000
Copper	63,150
Fluorite	1,180,955
Graphite	50,916
Lead	156,852
Manganese	96,081
Mercury	1,220
Sulphur	1,178,454
Tin	479
Tungsten	408
Zinc	264,972

and positive role in providing the basis for the production of sulphuric acid, the essential vehicle for a multitude of chemical reactions. In conjunction with Mexico's considerable reserves of petroleum, these materials offer considerable hope for the future for the development of a chemical industry in Mexico which will provide a much more sophisticated basis for its economy and further diversify the possible fields of employment for Mexicans.

PETROLEUM

Petroleum was known to the Aztecs, who called the black sticky stuff *chapopote,* and used it for ritual purposes. It was a Mexican who first sought to exploit the nation's petroleum resources in the mid-1890s, but lacking means of transportation and a domestic market which could absorb his product, he was unable to succeed. The first commercially successful well to be discovered in Mexico was located by an American oil company on 14 May 1901. This strike was made on privately owned land, and the Díaz government, concerned about the prospects of an American monopoly in an industry potentially so powerful, licensed rival companies, in particular the English company headed by Weetman D. Pearson, to exploit the oil-bearing potential of publicly owned lands under licence. Both sets of explorations were outstandingly successful, and at the time of World War I Mexican oilfields were the second most productive in the world. Throughout the years of the Revolution they continued to supply abundant quantities of oil from the oilfields around Tampico and in the Isthmus region to fuel the great mechanised war raging in Europe.

Undoubtedly, in the course of this frenetic exploration, there was a good deal of waste. In any case, waste was inseparable from the then rather primitive techniques of harnessing oil wells. Time and again fire broke out at oil wells, and some burnt out with a total loss; in 1920 one of the most productive of all Mexican oil wells suddenly turned to salt water, and at the time this was largely blamed on the exploitation of it for the European war. Under the Constitution of 1917 the Mexican government had already reasserted the claim which the Spanish government had made throughout the colonial times to the ownership of all minerals (including petroleum) located in the subsoil, regardless of the ownership of the land on the surface. Nevertheless, until the 1930s they continued to permit the existing companies to exploit the resources then available, and the formally British Mexican Eagle oil company went beyond this in opening up new fields which turned out to be as productive, if not more so, than any that had gone before. However, as a result of growing friction between the government of President Cárdenas and the American-owned oil companies, the provisions of the Constitution of 1917 were at last invoked. On 18 March 1938 President Cárdenas decreed nationalisation of all foreign-owned oil companies. Furthermore, when the governments of Britain and the United States demanded compensation, Mexicans gave freely and voluntarily to ensure that their national honour was upheld, and full compensation was paid punctually.

The immediate problems for the government in 1938 were considerable. The most important was that the foreign oil companies were able to prevent the sale abroad of Mexican oil to its traditional markets. However, Cárdenas, by barter deals and other agreements, was able to dispose of a reasonable exportable surplus, and the onset of the war soon made such limitations old fashioned. There remained the problem of inexperience and local unrest at home, but these difficulties, too, were overcome when in 1946 President Alemán installed a new and efficient administration in the state oil company Pemex. Through an intensive drive to reorganise the industry and find new sources of production, the nationalised industry had by 1952 again reached the levels of production it had not obtained since the early 1920s.

In recent years the state oil corporation has extended its activities successfully into the petrochemicals field. Plastics, synthetic rubber and detergents are among the finished products produced, as well as a wide range of raw materials for industry, all often implying a substantial saving on imports. Mexico's proved oil reserves have now been expanded to the point at which the country need fear no interruption in its domestic oil supplies for the foreseeable future, the proved reserves in 1972 exceeding 5,428 million barrels and 325·6 billion cubic metres of natural gas. The principal output comes from the north-eastern area around Tampico and from the Isthmus region, and the main producing fields now are those discovered by Pemex itself. The output of crude petroleum in 1971 was 28·2 million barrels. A total of twenty producing plants and fourteen state-owned oil refineries employ in all some 68,000 men. It is one of the problems of oil production that Mexico's output, although enormous, is not in itself of the correct quality to satisfy her domestic needs; a substantial proportion of crude oil and fuel oil is exported in order to pay for the import of petrol and paraffin, resulting in a net loss.

Natural gas, which is another aspect of Mexico's subsoil resources, is also under the control of Pemex and now contributes an important share to the national economy, being piped long distances into the industrial Core of Mexico from the oilfields. Production in 1971 was 18·22 million cubic metres.

ELECTRIC POWER

The initial development of electrical-power generation in Mexico was undertaken by private enterprise towards the end of the era of General Díaz, and involved the use of various modes of generation, of which the use of hydro-electric power from the plant at Necaxa Falls was one of the first. The dynamic entrepreneur behind the development of Mexico's electricity reserves, as behind much of her rail system, was Fred Stark Pearson, a Canadian who was killed in the sinking of the *Lusitania* in 1915. By 1960 installed capacity had reached 2·3 million kW and production exceeded 9,000 million kW, about half of it being produced by private enterprise and the other half by the Mexican government through the Federal Electricity Commission as part of its scheme to develop the less-advanced regions of Mexico.

In that year President López Mateos announced a major programme to double generating capacity within six years, and to this end to buy out the privately owned enterprises in order to facilitate any state investment in the electricity industry. The holdings of the two principal concerns were purchased outright without creating a premium demand and the governmental development programme went ahead without a hitch. In 1971 production of energy was 28,608 million kW. Half of the output (14,992 million kW) is still supplied from hydro-electric development, a fortunate product of

Mexico's many waterfalls. The remainder comes from a combination of oil-fired steam, diesel and internal-combustion plants. The fuel for the majority of these plants comes from Mexico's own hydrocarbon output. Mexico is also known to have substantial reserves of uranium, and has shown interest recently in the possible development of nuclear energy for power-production purposes.

CEMENT

Cement is a distinctive feature of the Mexican landscape. Not only is it widely used for posts and fencing, it also is used for water tanks and even sinks and wash-basins, for the use of lower-class Mexicans. Its production is one of the basic indicators of a modernising economy, and the demand for it as a building and roofing material in a country of dynamic population growth is of great importance. Cement was first produced in Mexico in 1906 by an American businessman, but the cement production of today is basically the creation of the 1920s. Major impetus was given to the industry by the large-scale public works of the Cárdenas regime. Its importance lies in the decentralisation it implies for the Mexican economy, and the fact that it enables the Mexican building industry to function.

TEXTILES

The first cotton mill was established by the Spaniards in Puebla as early as 1535, and throughout colonial times textiles was the major manufacturing industry. Mechanised production was introduced, again at Puebla, in 1830. The Díaz regime strongly encouraged textile production, and by 1910 output was able to satisfy domestic demand for all but the most expensive fabrics. Production continued to climb during the early years of the Revolution. However, by the

1930s the Mexican textile industry began to suffer from obsolescence, a problem which became increasingly acute. In the post-war period the arrival of artificial fabrics presented a new and serious challenge which the industry was too anachronistic to meet.

In the last twenty years, however, the situation has been considerably improved by the restraint imposed by the Mexican government on the import of textile machinery and this has enabled the existing factories to become more economical. The most important plants are still the cotton factories located in the Core region, a considerable distance from the cottonfields from which they draw their supplies. The production of wool textiles has also expanded enormously. Today, domestic production supplies a large measure of Mexico's continuously expanding textile needs.

TOURISM

Tourism is one of Mexico's largest industries, and has the considerable advantage over others that it is a major earner of foreign currency. In 1971 some 2·5 million tourists visited Mexico, and spent over $1,580 million. The vast majority of them came by air and spent most of their time in the Core region of Mexico, particularly in the capital. Tourist excursion programmes, however, also take in the west-coast holiday resort of Acapulco, the picturesque Indian culture of Oaxaca, and the antiquities of the Yucatán peninsula. In this way tourism plays an important role in distributing economic wealth throughout the country.

Mexican hotels, which are inspected by the government and subject to maximum tariffs, have been dramatically improved in recent years, and Mexico offers a wide range of accommodation suitable for all budgets. It is still a relatively inexpensive country to visit, even for a European, although the exchange rate, being tied to the American dollar, is artificially unfavourable for visitors from that part of the world. About a quarter of Mexico's total hotel accommodation is to be found in the Federal District, but there are adequate facilities in all the major tourist centres. It is an extremely competitive industry, and as a result is relatively efficient; its effect, moreover, is multiplied by the number of dependent services (restaurants, transportation, entertainment etc) which gain added momentum from the expansion of market which it implies.

Mexican tourism is in the care of an autonomous government department of tourism. It is this department which establishes hotel standards and sets the official maximum. In addition it provides good information centres where multilingual advice is readily available, and a range of publications giving information to the tourist; it also subsidises a number of privately owned tourist-information bulletins, such as *This Week* and *Mexico This Month*.

The most important development in recent years in Mexican tourism has been the establishment of a number of really first-rate hotels, but few can afford to patronise these. Their existence is vital in raising the general prestige of the hotel industry, and of setting standards which by a process of filtering down benefit the entire tourist industry. Although it is still possible to find traditional Spanish-type hostelries, and they are extremely cheap, Mexican hotels now expect to provide a breakfast service, lifts, iced-water machines and the other paraphernalia of modern Americanised living.

COMMERCE

No discussion of Mexican economic life would be meaningful without a concluding word on the enormous development in the sale and merchandising of products since World War II. Supermarket sales methods reached Mexico in 1945, and the introduction of standardised packaging, which supermarket sales implied, gave enormous impetus to a whole range of subsidiary industries. In the commercial field government enterprise has not yet arrived, but in 1947 the giant American discount house, Sears Roebuck, set up shop in Mexico City and created a powerful challenge to the old-fashioned Mexican businesses. Many of them have been dispersed entirely by the enormous chain of department stores, entirely Mexican owned, which go under the name of Salinas y Rocha (S & R). S & R began as a small department store in Monterrey in 1933, but in the early 1950s was revolutionised by American business methods, and sought its markets in middle- and lower-class Mexican patronage. Because they chose to concentrate on the most rapidly growing sector of Mexican purchasing power, S & R became the largest chain of its kind in the country. The improvements in methods which these large chains have pioneered have radically altered the entire field of retail selling in Mexico, and today it is possible to go into any small store and purchase a wide range of branded products which differ in few respects from those obtainable in Europe or the United States, but many of which are Mexican made. Standards of hygiene, cleanliness and courtesy are as high as anywhere in the world, and the Mexican government, in any case, has established modern standards of inspection for food, meat, milk and poultry, among others.

6

How They Get About

UNTIL recently, it was always difficult to get about in Mexico. In the time of the Aztecs, the Mexican economy depended almost entirely on man himself. Not only was he the most versatile animal for surmounting the many obstacles to travel, but in fact there was no feasible alternative that could carry anything like so much.

The Spaniards, who introduced the horse, were also responsible for the introduction of the much less spectacular and picturesque, but no less important, mule and donkey. The labouring masses of Mexico owe the Spaniards an untold debt for the amount of labour that these humble but essential beasts of burden have saved them. The mule or donkey became for many travellers, as for visitors to Spain itself, an essential part of the landscape. Today, it would certainly be rare to see these animals actually in use, unless one gets very far off the beaten track. However, they are still there, playing a necessary and useful role, but no longer do they form an essential part of the means of travel of all Mexicans.

Because the carriers were human, pre-Conquest communications had depended mainly on narrow trackways. For example, the Maya in Yucatán depended for the importation of jade (which was for them, as for the Chinese, the basis of their economy of exchange) on the importation of jadeite from the nearest available source—what is now Costa Rica. But the trackways along which the jade carriers must have moved have long since been obliterated by the jungle, and the only pre-Conquest highways of which we know today are the ceremonial ways built within the temple centres. Although magnificent enough, these roads were certainly not of great economic importance.

The Spaniards, as an organising power, built a system of highways, the *caminos reales*, which linked the various outposts of the vast empire of New Spain. These roads, which were built and paved in much the same style as those of the ancient Romans, were extremely durable and remained the foundation of the Mexican road system until the beginning of the present century, and sometimes later. The governments of the early republic paid all too little attention to roads, and after the war of French intervention and the rule of the Emperor Maximilian, it was the railways that attracted all the attention. In consequence, as in other countries in the late nineteenth century, Mexico enjoyed a railway-building boom, and they became the principal means of transport. To this day the smallest grade of village recorded for statistical purposes is known simply as a railway station (*estación del Ferrocarril*).

RAILWAYS

Because of its great altitude, the difficult gradients and the fact that it lies in a high valley, the construction of railways to and from Mexico City was an undertaking of considerable difficulty, and Mexico's first railroad, opened in 1864, was a short local line built by the French as part of their policy of supporting the empire. The first important line to leave the Valley of Mexico and to link the capital to the port of Vera Cruz was not completed until 1873. It was a difficult and dangerous journey, and remained so for many years. Derailments were frequent and accidents common.

For reasons of geographical convenience, therefore, the next major wave of railway building in Mexico was that linking the capital to the northern frontier. Here the first line built, the Mexican Central Railway, was able to leave the

Valley of Mexico through the Tajo de Nochistongo, a vast valley dug between 1607 and 1789 to drain the waters of the Valley of Mexico. The line from Mexico City to the frontier at Ciudad Juárez, some 1,200 miles away, was built in less than four years, and was followed by a wave of further railway building. Amalgamation of a number of these shorter lines brought about the linking of Mexico City to another point on the northern frontier, Nuevo Laredo. This was reconstructed in standard gauge by 1903, and became a popular route for communication between the United States and Mexico.

At the same time the first line was driven south of the capital into the state of Morelos and on to Oaxaca. This was difficult mountain territory, and the building of the line meant the construction of a great many tunnels and bridges across gorges. Despite this the wear and tear on the rolling stock was so great that it was always a very expensive line to run. South of this point there was a break in the system before one reached the Tehuantepec National Railway, a short line, only 188 miles long, joining the two sides of the Isthmus. The purpose of this line was primarily to serve as an interoceanic link, and the railway merely replaced the mule train that previously had carried goods across the frontier from the Atlantic to the Pacific coasts. Unfortunately, the line was badly built and had to be completely reconstructed. The British firm of S. Pearson & Son were called in for this purpose, but they did not take over the building and operation of the railroad until work had already begun on the Panama Canal, which was to render all other means of interoceanic communication obsolete. The TNR, however, did form the link between the main Mexican railway system and the short line to the south, the so-called Pan American Railway, which linked it to the Guatemalan frontier at Suchiate in 1913.

The problem of the railways was that they were always basically unsuitable as a means of linking valley settlements in the very mountainous country. The great majority of

Mexican railway mileage consisted of short lines, either feeding the product of mines into rather inadequate main-line systems, or else completely independent of them. Yet they did have one very important effect, which was to open up the desert north and to make it part of the national economy for the first time. One problem that arose was that it was in fact easier to link many parts of the north to the United States than to the rest of the country, and until 1927 the east coast was served only by a southward extension of the Southern Pacific Railroad of the United States. The completion of the link between this and the system of the Mexican national railways at Guadalajara then gave a unified transport system for the first time to the west coast. Finally, in 1955, the independent railway system of the state of Yucatán was finally linked to the rest of the system by a line running through the south of the state of Veracruz.

The governments of President Ruiz Cortines and López Mateos devoted a considerable amount of money to reconstructing the Mexican railroad system in a form that would make it an essential part of the modern economy. The track bed was strengthened, new rolling stock and powerful diesel locomotives were purchased. In 1937 the majority of the Mexican railways were nationalised, and in 1946 and 1950 the remaining lines were acquired through purchase. Today they are administered under the supervision of the ministry of communications through a number of semi-autonomous federal agencies. The majority of the systems are operated by Ferrocarriles Nacionales de México (FN de M). This controls almost all the main lines, with the only major exception of the independently administered Ferrocarril del Pacífico, which administers the line from Guadalajara north to the Mexican frontier at Nogales. The railways of the state of Yucatán are administered independently by that state, although they are linked to the rest of the system through a line, Ferrocarril de Sureste, which is administered directly by the ministry. Total mileage is 14,700 (23,400km). Freight handled amounts to something of the order of 25 million metric tonnes per annum.

Over 25 million passengers are carried annually, but it cannot be said that the railway is today a major passenger-carrying service. It has been displaced almost entirely by the numerous fleets of buses which ply Mexico's roads.

ROADS

By European standards, roads in Mexico today are quite adequate. Like the railways, the main long-distance roads run north and south, and carry a relatively light volume of traffic. It is in the area immediately surrounding the Valley of Mexico where large-scale modern road-building programmes have taken place, beginning with the autoroute from Mexico City to Puebla. In 1910 there were only a few miles of asphalt road, and, because of the disruption caused by the Revolution, in 1925 there was still only about 200 miles (320km) of all-weather road in the whole of Mexico. The coming of the automobile revolutionised this, and today there are some 92,369 miles (148,722km) of good roads.

Since 1950 the development of bus services has been dramatic. There are two sorts of bus: first-class buses which are modern and air conditioned running, as in the United States, between major cities with occasional stops for refreshments; and second-class buses. Second-class buses, which are often open-sided, range in appearance from the ramshackle to the utterly decrepit, and form the essential second rank in Mexican rural transportation. They are always incredibly crowded, and not just with people either. Licences to operate bus routes are awarded to Mexican firms only by the ministry of communications, and long-distance bus services are operated by competing companies with romantic names like Tres Estrellas or Transportes del Norte. First-class bus services are fast, convenient and reliable, and the tourist who wishes to get a good view of the country without too much discomfort is well advised to make use of them. There are altogether about 23,000 buses in Mexico.

Private motor transport, although widespread, is not of course as widespread as in the United States. Large American cars are very popular, especially among the *nouveaux riches*. The majority of Mexicans seem to prefer smaller continental models. The Volkswagen is particularly popular, as are the smaller Renaults and Fiats.

Urban traffic in Mexico, as in Spain, is fast and exciting; in the smaller towns, however, the paved stretch in the centre of the town often gives way to bad roads on the outskirts, and a multitude of pedestrians passing, stopping and conversing in the roadway as much as on the pavement, forces the driver to proceed with caution. There are currently about 500,000 private motor-cars in Mexico, representing about one for every ten of the population, so the Mexican car industry has a long way to go.

Realising the importance of this dynamic element in their rapidly growing economy, the Mexican government have taken steps to ensure that the market is well maintained, and some years ago purchased the Borgward plant complete from East Germany in order to assemble all-Mexican cars in Monterrey. This programme ran into economic difficulties, but Mexico remains one of only two Latin American countries actually manufacturing automobiles from scratch, as opposed to merely assembling imported vehicles. Even more important is the Mexican truck industry, which has done so much in recent years to bring the outlying districts within the national economy. Like bus companies, trucking companies depend on concessions from the ministry of communications, and the driving of trucks is restricted on Mexican highways to Mexicans.

AIR

The combination of mountain and desert which is characteristic of Mexico makes air travel the logical way of getting

NATIONAL AIR ROUTES

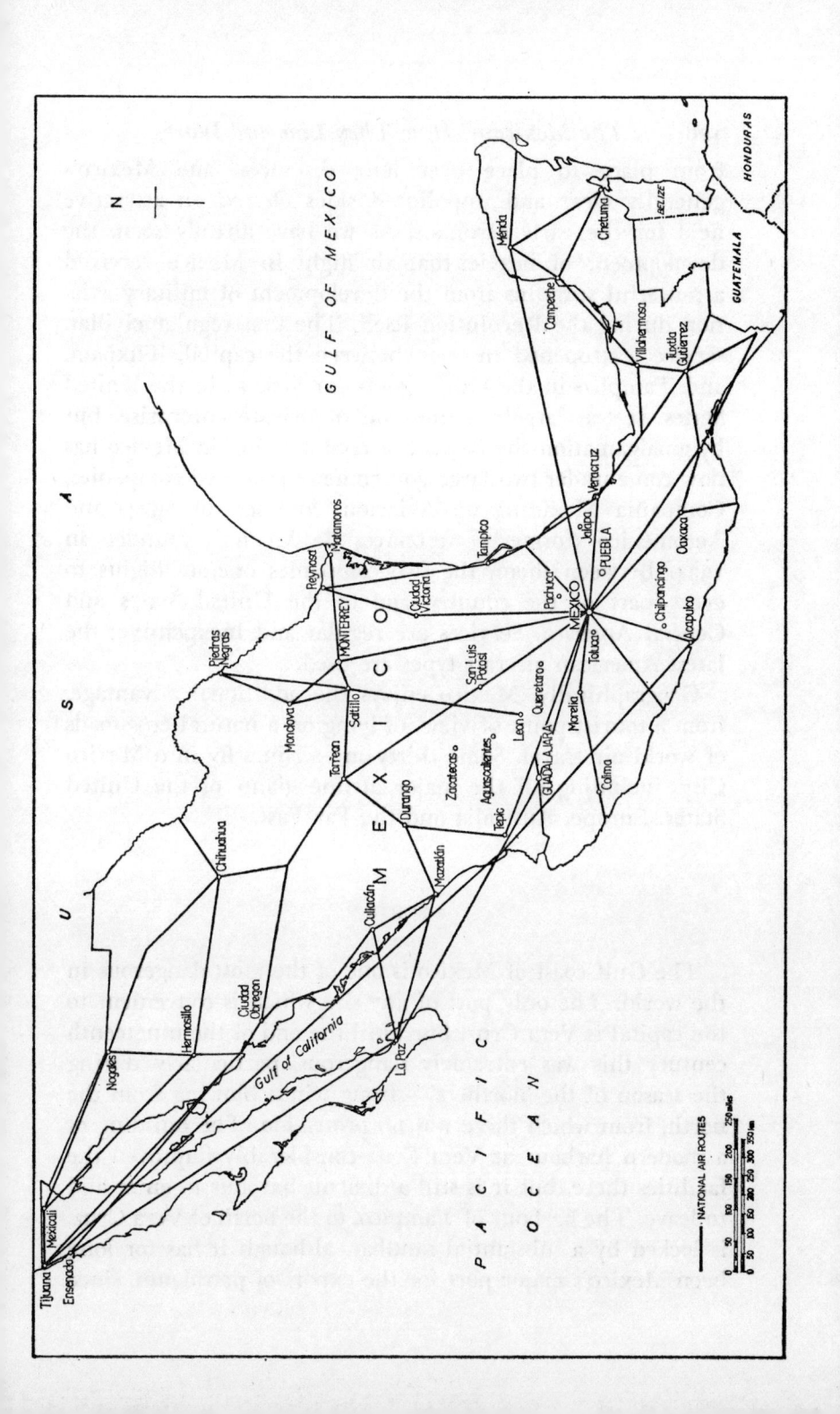

from place to place over long distances, and Mexico's generally clear and unpolluted skies offered an attractive field for the early aeronaut. As we have already seen, the development of heavier-than-air flight in Mexico received a powerful stimulus from the development of military aviation during the Revolution itself. The first regular civilian service was opened in 1920 between the capital, Tuxpam, and Tampico in the Gulf region. At first, as in the United States, it was largely a question of private enterprise, but by amalgamation the control of civil aviation in Mexico has now come under two large government-sponsored companies, Compañia Mexicana de Aviación, founded in 1924, and Aeroméxico (formerly Aeronaves de México), founded in 1934. Between them, the two companies operate flights to every part of the country and to the United States and Central America. Services are regular and inexpensive; the latest American aircraft types are used.

Geographically, Mexico enjoys the additional advantage, from a tourist point of view, of lying on a natural crossroads of world air travel. Some thirty-one airlines fly into Mexico City, including all the major airline giants of the United States, Europe, Australia and the Far East.

PORTS

The Gulf coast of Mexico is one of the most dangerous in the world. The only port of any size which is convenient to the capital is Vera Cruz, but until the end of the nineteenth century this was extremely dangerous, particularly during the season of the 'northers'—strong winds blowing from the north, from which there was no protection. The building of a modern harbour at Vera Cruz considerably improved the facilities there, but it is still a difficult harbour to enter and to leave. The harbour of Tampico, to the north of Vera Cruz, is locked by a substantial sandbar, although it has for long been Mexico's major port for the export of petroleum, since it lies immediately adjacent to the large Tampico oilfield. To the south, the port of Frontera in Tabasco is little more than a fishing village. Progreso, the port for Mérida in Yucatán, is thriving today under the revival of the economy of Yucatán; its principal significance lies in its exports of *henequén* or sisal. The port of Coatzacoalcos in the Isthmus is a small town which acts as the terminal for the railway and road joining the two oceans; it is not in itself important, but it lies at the mouth of the river which is navigable by ocean-going vessels for the 24 miles (38·6km) up to Minatitlán, the seat of a large oil refinery which serves the Isthmian oilfield. Of all the Atlantic ports, only Vera Cruz is now of any significance as a passenger port for services from Italy and Spain. The Hamburg–America Line, which sails from Bremen and Antwerp to Vera Cruz, also continues to Tampico.

On the Pacific coast, however, the situation is rather different. Here the most important port, and one of the best known cities in Mexico, is the resort of Acapulco. The city's importance is relatively recent since it has very mountainous country lying immediately behind it and was of no great value as a port until after World War II. However, the development and improvement of the road from Mexico City via Cuernavaca and Taxco has changed all that. P & O's large ships call at Acapulco on their way to and from Europe, and the journey to their port from Southampton and Le Havre by way of the Panama Canal is by far the easiest way for the tourist to reach Mexico by sea. German and Italian ships passing through the Canal also call at Acapulco. To the north of Acapulco, Mazatlán and Guaymas in the state of Sonora are important cargo ports for exports from the northern states, although a large proportion of Mexico's exports leave the country over the land frontier with the United States, as might be expected.

TRAFFIC

Most visitors will probably get their first impression of Mexican traffic from the capital. As already mentioned, driving in this as in other major cities is vigorous and rapid, and the problem of traffic congestion in the capital is, because of its size, a considerable one. Starting in the late 1960s, the government has made a major attempt to alleviate the congestion by the construction of a new underground railway, the Metro. Built on the French system, with attractive square cars running on rubber-tyred wheels, this is an extremely comfortable way to travel, but it is a rather impersonal way to get about.

The buses of the capital are extremely numerous and cheap, although one regrets the disappearance of the picturesque old trams which ran on special tracks in the middle of the roadway and were the basis for the extraordinary growth of the capital. Many Mexicans, as well as visitors, make use of the many taxis which are similarly inexpensive. An interesting Mexican institution is the so-called *Pesero*. On the two main intersecting avenues of Mexico City, namely the Paséo de la Reforma and the Insurgentes, one sees taxis passing with the driver holding one hand out of the window in a drooping attitude. This indicates that his is a communal taxi in which anyone can travel any distance along a set route for the fee of one peso. They are often small cars and the inside is extremely crowded, but everyone is very friendly and they are an excellent way to travel.

Pollution, resulting from the very large number of motorcars, is an acute problem in the capital. The high altitude of Mexico City and the fact that it lies in a basin exacerbates matters.

However, it must be pointed out that the enormous concentration of motor vehicles in and around the capital means that motoring is relatively trouble-free in most of the rest of the country, although modern high-compression engines tend to be rather sluggish in the altitudes encountered. Scenery varies from the excellent to the absolutely spectacular, and the greatest danger to the traveller in Mexico is maintaining an adequate degree of concentration on the task in hand, particularly on mountain roads where the bends are extremely sharp and oncoming vehicles may be travelling at very considerable speed. It is quite common to see small boys holding up things to eat for passers-by to purchase should they feel so inclined. The most disconcerting is the popular iguana, a Mexican reptile, the flesh of which when cooked tastes rather like chicken and is regarded as a great delicacy.

Road mileage with all-weather surface totalled about 36,423 (58,278km) in 1970. The principal highway runs from the United States border to Mexico City and then south as far as the Guatemalan border; the first part of this was opened in 1936 and the extension completed in 1950. All but a very short section of it—where it enters the city—is single carriageway. South of the city a fine new motorway has been constructed leading southward into the state of Morelos, taking a longer and lower route around the mountain slopes than the old highway to Cuernavaca. All these roads are of good quality, and it is possible to maintain high average speeds on them. Where speeding is discouraged, however, the Mexicans frequently have resort to the ingenious device of laying corrugated strips of concrete or large metal studs in the road. These obstacles, which are known as 'sleeping policemen', are alarmingly effective and should be negotiated with extreme caution.

Where permitted, parking is frequently supervised by uniformed car watchers, who should be tipped a peso. (Filling station attendants, too, whom it is advisable to watch very closely, generally get no regular salary and expect a tip for their trouble.) Parking and other motoring offences are dealt with by the traffic police—a separate and distinct force, who wear dark-brown shirts and khaki trousers with a white belt and, in addition to the revolver which all Mexican police carry, also carry a screwdriver. They use this to unscrew the licence plates of any car found illegally parked. In order to recover them and be allowed legally to drive off, one must first of all pay one's fine at the traffic office.

Licence holders are subject not only to a driving test but also to a regular annual medical inspection. Foreign visitors, however, unless resident in Mexico, can drive on a United States driving licence or a valid International Driving Permit.

Outside the cities the principal roads are patrolled twice a day, six days a week, by the so-called 'Green Angels'—radio-equipped patrol cars able to handle minor repairs, give first-aid or answer questions. To flag them down, when stopped by the side of the road, raise the bonnet (hood) of your car.

MAIL AND TELEPHONE

As befits a gregarious people, Mexicans exchange a great deal of correspondence and post offices are busy and cheerful places. In 1971 Mexicans exchanged 907 million items of mail, and received 259 million letters from abroad. It may or may not be significant that they dispatched overseas only 200 million replies!

The development of the telephone in Mexico was for a long while retarded by the existence of not one but two rival systems, one American and the other Swedish. Today they have been consolidated into a single system, Teléfonos de México, and, despite the jokes Mexicans themselves make about the system, it appears to work as well as most. Telephones are mainly used by business and commercial enterprises, who make up the bulk of the subscribers. There are 1,712,000 instruments in use, or 3.4 for every 100 inhabitants. Public telephones are, as in the United States, frequently located in the entry of cafés or stores, and not in the street.

There is a good telegraph service, with three rates depending on the class and speed of service desired. All domestic rates are low and visitors frequently find it advisable to use the fastest (*Extra Urgente*). Overseas cables are handled by the Mexican service to the frontier, thereafter by Western Union.

7

How They Learn

MEXICAN education is one of the great success stories of the Revolution. It forms the largest single item in the national budget, about 25 per cent, and it is one subject upon which almost all Mexicans are agreed. This has not always been so. The reason for this is that under Spanish colonial rule education was largely in the hands of the church, and the fathers of Mexican independence were as much opposed to the continued clerical dominance in education as they were to continued Spanish rule. The wars and conflicts of the nineteenth century, culminating in the programme of the Reform, left a legacy of bitterness which took generations to erase. Under Díaz the church began to reassert itself, and as a result militant anti-clericalism was a feature of the middle years of the Revolution, during which clerical schools were suppressed and the principle was established that the state, and the state alone, was wholly responsible for education.

Although there was certainly education in Mexico before the coming of the Spaniards, and indeed the presence of several high-level pre-Columbian cultures indicates the degree of sophistication of the educational processes of the ruling and priestly classes, the Spaniards were the founders of education in Mexico in the modern sense—and, as they did in other fields, they gave the Mexicans the best they had to offer. The friars who came to Mexico with Cortés originated the instruction of the Indians and formal primary instruction began in 1523. The further development of education in Mexico was largely in the hands of teaching orders, and their work culminated in the foundation of the University of Mexico in 1551. Other landmarks were the opening of a training school for teachers, and in the last years of Spanish rule, the founding of the School of Mines in 1792. This last was one of the first institutions of technical education in the Americas, and at the time of its foundation one of the most advanced in the world.

The struggles of the Reform left Mexican education in a sorry state. Many schools had been closed, as had four of Mexico's six universities. In 1867 the government of the restored republic founded the National Preparatory School, which became the centre of higher education for a generation. It was strongly committed ideologically to the positivism of Auguste Comte, and to the deliberate refashioning of Mexican society—and for this the positivists were prepared to accept the powerful dictatorship of General Díaz. The dictatorship failed to justify the expectations which they placed in it, but it did succeed in producing substantial advances in education, although in a narrow-minded and often unsatisfactory way. In 1893 national legislation provided for universal compulsory free education for the first time; it was, however, a hope only, and at most one-fifth of the eligible school population received some form of instruction at primary level.

One of the last acts of the Díaz administration was to refound the National University, which had been in abeyance since the days of the Reform. Although during the early violent years of the Revolution activity there dwindled almost to nothing, it nevertheless survived to form the basis of Mexican higher education today. Far more serious was the impact of the Revolution on primary and secondary education. What it amounted to was that the government of General Obregón (1920-4) was faced with the need completely to reconstruct from the beginning. For this purpose he reconstituted the Ministry of Public Instruction, and appointed to it one of the most famous names in Mexican educational history, that of José Vasconcelos. As minister of public instruction Vasconcelos was a dynamic figure who enjoyed the full backing of the first stable government Mexico had enjoyed since the days of Díaz, and he poured his energies into the reconstruction of primary schools. All kinds of ingenious devices were used to drive home the message of education. In poor neighbourhoods showplace schools were set up, free meals were given to poor children who were thus enabled to reach education for the first time, students were encouraged to go out into the countryside to teach literacy to older people who had missed the opportunity of education in youth, free reprints of the great classics were distributed widely, and made available to people who had never before had the chance to read good literature. Most spectacularly, Vasconcelos gave the walls of public buildings over to the rising generation of Mexican mural artists who covered them with enormous and brash paintings depicting the advances of the revolution and the hopes for the Mexican future. Vasconcelos himself fell foul of the leadings lights of the National University, and resigned in 1923, but the work of education went on, and despite the enormous growth of the Mexican population in recent years it continues to hold its own against all difficulties.

TABLE 5: EDUCATION 1969-70

	Schools	Teachers	Pupils
Kindergarten	2,910	11,493	378,098
Primary	42,815	173,615	8,766,081
Secondary	2,437	56,324	786,105
Pre-university	334	9,052	96,408
Commercial	705	6,414	92,415
Teacher training	235	7,329	65,712
Professional and special	778	15,805	198,201

PRIMARY EDUCATION

Free primary education is open to all Mexicans between six and fourteen. There are about 43,815 primary schools in Mexico and 173,615 teachers engaged in primary education. In 1969 there were 8,766,081 pupils in primary education. Owing to the wide dispersion of the rural Mexican population in small villages and hamlets, there is a considerable disparity between the size and range of schools in rural and in urban areas. In general rural schools provide for only the first two or three grades, and seldom more than four. Boys and girls who have the ability and the encouragement to proceed beyond these grades have to go to the nearest town. Since very few do so, this means that the Mexican educational system is still troubled by the loss of a great many children after the second grade (seven to eight). These children, who start agricultural or other work immediately afterwards, become adults who are in effect illiterate, and hence a great deal of effort has to be spent on rectifying this situation when they reach maturity. In the urban areas on the other hand congestion is serious, and the average teacher/pupil ratio is one to forty-seven.

The syllabus of primary education is uniform throughout Mexico, both for public schools and for private schools, of which there are about 2,000. Private education is permitted, and accounts for some 9 per cent of all primary education, but clerical education is not and church bodies are strictly forbidden to organise religious education in any way whatsoever. The educational scheme lays heavy emphasis on the civic and social responsibilities of the children and makes a very definite effort to ensure that Mexicans are aware of not only their opportunities but also of their responsibilities. The socialisation of Mexico's youth, however, is most effectively accomplished by the fact that all instruction is given through the medium of the Spanish language. It is the acquisition of this language that makes a child a Mexican.

Pre-primary education is fairly widespread. In 1969 there were 2,910 institutions giving pre-school instruction, with 11,493 teachers and 378,098 pupils.

TABLE 6: MEDIAN OF EDUCATIONAL ATTAINMENT

Age group	Years of formal schooling
15–19	4·41
20–29	4·13
30–39	3·85
Over 40	3·71

SECONDARY EDUCATION

Secondary education in Mexico begins at the age of twelve, is organised on the basis of a three-, six- or nine-year cycle and, broadly speaking, is divided into two categories. On the one hand there is preparatory education (three plus three years), by which is meant education designed to prepare the student for future higher education at university level. Students who complete the cycle of secondary education, therefore, proceed to courses at university level in law, medicine, dentistry, veterinary science, economics or engineering. They may also undertake the study of the social sciences or arts. This, however, accounts for a relatively small proportion of the whole, and once more a great many of those who complete secondary education do not go on to further study at this sort of level. A small proportion of girls go on to careers in nursing or social work and boys may enter the military system of education and work towards a career in the Forces.

The other great branch of the secondary educational system is described as 'vocational' (three plus six years). This is designed to prepare candidates not for the universities but for distinct institutions which will instruct them for specific careers in science or engineering. It is very difficult from the official statistics to determine exactly how many students go into each branch of the secondary system, but it is clear that the largest single proportion of the total output goes into commerce. Current enrolment in secondary education as a whole runs at something in excess of 1,483,800. This represents at most about 11 per cent of the total age group potentially eligible for secondary education (net enrolment ratio, 1970). In 1950 only about 2·6 per cent of all Mexicans had completed a period of secondary education, and only 1·4 per cent had completed the necessary entrance qualifications for admittance into higher education. The pressure on primary education since has meant that these figures have not risen as much as could have been hoped, but it is still a great achievement even to have maintained this proportion.

TECHNICAL

As in most developing countries, technical education is the most pressing need for Mexico, in order to give the country the educated force of specialists which it requires to maintain its growth. In 1970 Mexico had only 0·8 scientists and engineers for each 10,000 of the population, and only 0·1 technicians. There are numerous institutes striving to rectify this—both federal and state supported, as well as a number of private ones.

The most celebrated of these last is the National Technical Institute at Monterrey in northern Mexico. The state-supported institutions are responsible for the great bulk of the commercial and vocational education given in the country.

At the apex of the technical system stands the Instituto Politecnico Nacional founded by President Cárdenas in 1936. It is situated in a wholesome precinct in the Tlatelolco district of Mexico City, with its centre on the Plaza de Tres Culturas. It is this institution that has taken the bulk of the expansion of higher education in Mexico in the course of the last fifteen years, and it is because it has received relatively less support from the government than the more favoured university sector that the students of the Politecnico feel that they have a special grievance. Currently there are over 50,000 students housed in an institution designed to cater for half that number, with something like an equivalent number in various institutes supervised by the Politecnico indirectly. The Politecnico is particularly distinguished for its output of engineers and architects, disciplines in which Mexicans have proved themselves outstanding.

UNIVERSITY

At the apex of the Mexican university system, and of the educational system of the country as a whole, stands the National Autonomous University of Mexico, commonly abbreviated UNAM. Its name derives from the fact that in 1929 it was granted autonomy, that is to say the ability to run its own internal affairs, and by law it is a public corporation separate from the state. In this respect it contrasts with the Politecnico which is directly under the control of the minister of education.

The university grew out of those faculties of the original Royal University of Mexico which survived the closure of the Reform, and which were reconstituted as the National University in 1910. Its premises in the old centre of the capital, close to the Zócalo, proved inadequate in the 1920s and 1930s, and under the administration of President Alemán, a new university city was constructed some 14 miles outside the city centre. The university moved there in 1953, although library and some other facilities were retained on the old site. The campus itself, with its dramatic murals and shady walkways, is an architectural storehouse of great importance. No effort was spared to make it a showplace worthy of the Mexican people, and murals which are displayed on every available wall surface tell the story of how the Mexican people came to express themselves in modern terms.

Among other noteworthy buildings the Faculty of Arts stands out because it is more than a quarter of a mile long. Most visitors, however, are struck immediately by the tall eight-storey windowless tower of the university library, which is covered with murals on all four sides by the artist Juan O'Gorman. The sciences are catered for with a number of specially planned laboratory buildings of which the Cosmic Ray Pavilion, designed by the architect Félix Candela, is the most celebrated. The physical aspects of education are not neglected either. The enormous Olympic Stadium, now enlarged to hold 100,000 spectators, immediately adjoins it and is connected to it by easily negotiated ramps. It, too, is ornamented with dramatic murals. The university enjoys excellent communications, and in particular its own bus station, the services from which to the centre of the city are subsidised by the government to hold them down to a reasonable price.

There are three other universities in the capital itself, and eleven more run by various of the states, two of which are in the state of Jalisco. The range of courses offered by these institutions is, of course, more limited than at the UNAM. However, they enjoy the same opportunity for the cultivation of the spirit of free enquiry which characterises their senior partner in the university system. Pictures of tanks on the campus at the National University during the student disturbances in 1968 were shocking to Mexicans precisely because the spectacle had been unknown for so long, and it is very probable that it will not recur. The university is administered by a rector who is elected for a four-year term by a governing body which includes student representatives. The job of the rector is not an easy one, wedged in as he is between some of the world's most militant students and a government deeply conscious of the many competing demands for resources. The students in the major institutions of higher education in Mexico are on the whole very left wing, not only because of the natural feeling that more could be done to better the lot of their fellows, but also by deliberate training and tradition inculcated by the history of the Revolution itself.

On the other hand, students, particularly at the Autonomous University, are extremely well looked after. A university crêche is available to look after the children of the many married students and employees. Prices in the cafeterias and restaurants and in the many shops of the university city are controlled and subsidised. There is a highly sophisticated job-placement service, and all students are given free medical treatment and subjected to regular compulsory medical examinations.

FURTHER EDUCATION

Further education in Mexico is based on the principle of cultural diffusion. At its centre is the UNAM itself. The purpose of the university, in fact, is not merely to provide a place to which students can come, but also to provide a centre from which teaching may be sent outwards. The most spectacular evidence of this is the existence of the Radio University. This broadcasts daily from 8 am until midnight, and deals with every aspect of Mexican culture including art, the cinema and the theatre. Its tuition programmes, which are of university standard, are supplemented by audiovisual materials, as well as the museum in Chapultepec park and a pavilion where the inhabitants of the capital can read, listen to music, lectures and recitals, and take free courses in various subjects.

At the other end of the scale there is still great embarrassment about the fact that according to official statistics, which for Mexico are usually most reliable, there is probably still something like 30 per cent of the population above the age of five who are illiterate. When they have to communicate with their relatives in distant villages or towns, many poor people have recourse to public letter writers, and in the capital there is a whole street of them, each sitting at a little table with its own typewriter. This shame is misplaced. Illiteracy results from a lack of educational opportunity, not from a lack of intelligence, and the fact that so many Mexicans cannot read or write is a product of the past history of the country and not of themselves. Mexicans, without being in any way complacent, can be justifiably proud of how far they have already come. In 1910 the census showed 76.9 per cent of all Mexicans were illiterate; by 1960 the proportion had been reduced to 37.8 per cent. The lowest rate of illiteracy, as would be expected, is to be found in the Federal District where only 16 per cent were recorded as illiterate; the highest figure comes from the state of Guerrero, where the extremely broken nature of the countryside and very small communities make it difficult to maintain an adequate school system in an area in which children have traditionally been required to work on the land as soon as they were able to be of any use. In actual numbers the figures for the nation as a whole are roughly the same, namely somewhere in the region of 11 million people. It should be remembered, however, that of these over 3 million people speak only an Indian language and relatively few of these have a written form.

8

How They Amuse Themselves

SOCIAL life for Mexican men revolves around the café. It is here that they meet and talk, either for the purpose of discussing business or purely for amusement. Not that women are wholly excluded from café life; however, no unmarried woman participates in it outside the big cities and no married woman would be present at one without her husband.

Cafés and other eating establishments are frequent in any urban settlement in Mexico. Often they are open-fronted, although an arcaded sidewalk separates them from the dusty and frequently unmade road. Café life, too, goes on throughout the day, but cafés will be particularly crowded at meal times when it may be quite impossible for a visitor to get a seat. More affluent Mexicans patronise *pâtisseries* on the French model. Foreign-owned restaurants offering a wide range of cuisine are a feature of larger cities, and in the capital it is possible to eat the individual cuisine of almost every other country in Europe or the Americas.

The sharpest division between the well-to-do and the poorer classes, however, comes in the consumption of alcohol. The more affluent Mexicans—and most foreign tourists—patronise bars on the American model. The poorer Mexicans frequent the numerous romantically named *pulquerías*, where the national drink, the fermented juice of the maguey cactus, is served.

Dining out in other people's homes is not characteristically Mexican, but the home is the focus of female social life, and it is common to see them sitting around in their spacious patios or courtyards, discussing the day. As in Spain, it is customary to gather for social conversation well before the evening meal, and a great deal of time in every day is spent in this fashion.

Well-to-do Mexicans frequently have weekend homes. Lake Patzcuaro in Morelos is a favourite locale for these, but there are many others. The cooler air of the mountains is particularly attractive to those who reside in the capital, while those who live in the steamy lowlands will tend to treat the capital itself as their retreat from the damp and the heat. Many of the inhabitants of the capital, of all classes, go to Chapultepec park on Sundays, and pass the time strolling or picnicking beneath the trees. Others still make the journey out to Xochimilco, where the so-called 'floating gardens' consist of the last remnant of Lake Texcoco, with its banks formed by artificial platforms covered with earth on the model of the ancient Aztec settlement of Tenochtitlan itself. The canals of Xochimilco are covered with brightly coloured punts with awnings decorated with flowers, and they pass and re-pass each other with great solemnity. Many of them are crowded to the brim with Mexican families enjoying the picnic; others with visiting tourists with clicking cameras. Bands playing from the larger punts enliven the air, for Mexicans seldom go anywhere where they are out of reach of music.

FIESTAS

Fiesta is the Mexican name for the jollity and merrymaking inseparable from any important public holiday. Every day in Mexico is a holiday somewhere. Most of them are important dates in the religious calendar, the anniversaries of saints or of some great national event. Furthermore, some of the saints' festivals involve ceremonies which go well back before the arrival of Cortés, while on the other hand many of the secular festivals are also celebrated with the traditional music, ritual, eating and drinking, fireworks, and other forms of public rejoicing traditionally associated with the days of the saints.

Easter is an especially important festival. On the Saturday of Holy Week a particularly unusual ceremony, peculiar to that country, is held in many parts of Mexico. In order to make the children grow, adults lift them into the air by their ears, and then give them a sound beating with branches. Today they are taught that this is to teach them to obey their parents and God; its resemblance to a pre-Columbian nature festival is obvious. The famous 'bird men' (*Voladores*) of Oaxaca, who spin round a tall pole attached to the end of fibre ropes, similarly recall the animistic basis of pre-Columbian religion.

Christmas, too, is celebrated in Mexico with elaborate ceremony, starting on 16 December and lasting for a period of nine days, which are known in Spanish as the *posadas*. A *posada* is a Spanish inn, and the name refers to the journey of Joseph and Mary up to Bethlehem. Mexicans take it in turn to offer hospitality to one another during these days, but they do not simply invite their friends in. The place for the night's festivities having been decided upon in advance, small processions form led by children carrying candles, and these proceed from one house to another, at each of which they are turned away in a ritual musical exchange. At the selected house they are permitted to enter, and prayers are held before the festivity begins. The climax of the evening is the smashing of an enormous brightly decorated jar containing presents for the children.

More macabre is the festival enacted throughout Mexico on the Day of the Dead, that is to say the feast of All Souls on 2 November. Death, as every visitor to Mexico rapidly discovers, played a dominant part in Aztec and Toltec religion, and the ceremony of reunion with the spirits of the departed has been transferred to this Christian festival. Every confectioner and pastry shop displays characteristic sweetmeats made of sugar or dough formed in the shape of skulls. Presents are also made in the shape of coffins containing skeletons which are exchanged between children. Also on the Day of the Dead families go out to the graveyards where their relatives are buried, taking with them gifts for the deceased as well as the flowers and candles associated with religious ceremonies. After prayers families may remain to picnic in the graveyards, and on their return home in the evening it is customary to serve meals containing those dishes of which the dead were known to be particularly fond.

The only Mexican-born saint, St Felipe Jesús, is celebrated on 5 February with elaborate religious ceremonies. Although officially the state is secular and does not recognise religious holidays, on that day, which is also Constitution Day, all government offices are closed. Instead the churches are crowded and each member of the congregation carries a sprig of greenery in memory of the Resurrection. St Felipe himself was a Franciscan monk who was shipwrecked on the coast of Japan and crucified in Nagasaki by order of the emperor in the year 1597. Relics of him are preserved in the cathedral in Mexico City.

Secular holidays include such events as the victory of the Mexicans over the French, which is celebrated on 5 May, and the birthday of Benito Juárez. But the most important celebration of the year is that on 16 September of the Grito de Dolores—the day on which Father Hidalgo proclaimed Mexican independence in 1810. On this day the president of Mexico appears on the balcony of the National Palace, and before an enormous crowd which throngs the Zócalo solemnly rings the bell which once hung in the parish church at Dolores, and now hangs in the central balcony of the main front of the palace. Table 7 lists statutory public holidays. The following festivals, although optional, are also widely celebrated throughout Mexico: 6 January (Day of the Three Kings); 17 January (Blessing of the Animals); 2 February (Candelaria Day); 3 May (Day of the Holy Cross); 24 June (St John the Baptist); 15 August (Feast of the Assumption); 15 September, 4 October (Feast of St Francis); 12 October (Day of the Race—Columbus Day); 1–2 November (All Souls and All Saints Days); 12 December (Guadalupe Day); 16–24 December (Posadas); 28 December (Innocents Day); 31 December (New Year's Eve)

TABLE 7: STATUTORY PUBLIC HOLIDAYS IN MEXICO

Date	Description or title
1 January	New Year's Day
5 February	Constitution Day
21 March	Birthday of Benito Juárez
1 May	Labour Day
5 May	Anniversary of the Battle of Puebla
1 September	National Holiday. State of the Union Report
16 September	Independence Day
30 September	Anniversary of the birth of Morelos
20 November	Anniversary of the Mexican Ievolution, 1910
25 December	Christmas Day

BULLFIGHTING

The great event of the Mexican Sunday afternoon is the bullfight. In the enormous bullring of Mexico City, with a capacity of 50,000 spectators, the *corrida* begins promptly at 4 pm. The forms and the ceremonies of Mexican bullfights are exactly the same as in Spain, although the bulls themselves are Mexican bred and *aficionados* say that they are less lively and slightly less dangerous. Their breeders, who maintain between them more than ninety stud farms, are organised into The Association of Breeders of Fighting Bulls, and they supply more than 1,000 every year for combat.

It is not known exactly how early bullfighting was introduced into Mexico; the first recorded fight was held in 1529, but before that time Cortés himself had had a bullring constructed for his private entertainment on his country estate, and presumably fights had been held there. The sport received great encouragement from Mexico's second bullring, the Plaza del Volador, which was constructed on the orders of the then Archbishop of Mexico so that he and subsequent viceroys could watch the sport from the National Palace itself; and in 1787 the cost of building Chapultepec was met in part by the institution of an annual bullfight. The present Plaza México was built and inaugurated in 1946 and is by far the largest in the world. Incidentally, the name of the Plaza del Volador refers to the flying ritual of the Indians of Oaxaca, already referred to, which at one time was widespread throughout Mexico.

OTHER SPORTS

As in other Spanish speaking countries, bullfighting is beginning to yield something of its former popularity to a much more widely practised sport, namely soccer. Its relative cheapness, and the fact that it is readily available to hundreds of thousands of poor boys who stand no chance whatsoever of being able to demonstrate their skill with the bull, means that it has become extremely popular. The choice of Mexico as the first Latin American country to stage the World Cup in 1970 followed naturally.

The playing of ball games, however, has a much more ancient history in Mexico. The Maya played an elaborate ritual ball game with religious significance, for the purpose of which enormous ball courts were constructed. Those of Chichén Itzá are among the most celebrated. The ball, which could only be struck by the heels, ankles or wrists, was made of natural rubber in strands and it had to be propelled through a small ring set high up on the wall on one side of the court. Recently archaeologists pointed out that the situation of the ring and its thickness make it exceedingly unlikely that either side was ever able to score, so that the ceremony must have been something like the

Eton Wall Game. This was fortunate, since murals on the side of the court make it quite clear that the captain of the losing team was beheaded.

Mexicans still enjoy the peculiarly Mexican sport called jai-alai, a game which is somewhat similar to squash but bears a closer family resemblance to the Basque game of pelota. Played on an indoor court, this is believed to be the fastest game in the world, the ball at times reaching a speed in excess of 150 miles (241·5km) an hour. The arena itself is floored with concrete; the wall is constructed of granite blocks so as to withstand the punishing effect of the impact. The ball itself, which is made of goatskin and linen thread around a core of rubber, is propelled from a wickerwork basket strapped to the right arm.

In view of the country's proximity to the United States, it is not surprising that Mexicans also play baseball, although the sport is not as popular as it is in some other Latin American countries. Considerable interest is taken in athletics, as in swimming and diving, and indeed there are few sports played anywhere in the world in which Mexicans do not take part.

THE CINEMA

Mexicans are enthusiastic cinemagoers. In 1970 there were 1,765 permanent cinemas in the country, with a total of 1,496,000 seats—or 30 seats for every 1,000 of the population. Attendances were recorded at 251·5 million—an average of five per year per person, a figure equal to that of the United States and more than double that for the UK. An important factor contributing to the popularity of the cinema in Mexico is the strength of the national film industry. Not only is this preponderant within its own country, but it also exercises a powerful influence on that of the Spanish-speaking world as a whole, and its leading stars and directors have international reputations.

The cinema was introduced to Mexico in 1897 by a young

engineer named Salvador Toscano, who sold his stamp-collection to buy one of the first hand-cranked cameras from the Lumière brothers in Paris. With an eye to the commercial possibilities of footage of important public ceremonies, he recorded the great days of the last years of the Díaz regime—military parades, the opening of the Tehuantepec National Railroad, and the celebrations of the centennial. Then came the Revolution. Despite the difficulties of the unwieldy hand-cranked machines of the day, Toscano took to the railways to record precious footage of the great scenes of the Revolution: the fall of Díaz, the arrival of Madero, the coup of General Huerta and the endless battles. Much later it was edited by his daughter, Señora Carmen Toscano de Moreno Sánchez, into a great picaresque narrative of the Revolution itself, entitled *Memorias de un Mexicano* (1947).

The first non-documentary film made in Mexico was a one-reeler called *Don Juan Tenorio*, produced by Toscano in 1898. After the turn of the century the new medium attracted rivals, both as exhibitors and as directors. It was not until 1915 that the first full-length feature film was attempted, but the next eight years, despite continued war and uncertainty, saw the first flowering of the native Mexican cinema. By the end of this period the huge output of Hollywood was already dominating the world scene—an ascendancy firmly established by the appearance of the 'talkie' in 1926, with its demands for enormously greater resources and more elaborate sets. Yet with directors such as Raphael J. Sevilla and Antonio Moreno the Mexican cinema was firmly established in the new medium by the beginning of the 1930s. From only 6 films in 1932, output leapt to 20 in 1933 and continued to rise to 57 in 1938, partly under the impetus of government encouragement, partly from the excitement generated by the arrival of Sergei Eisenstein, whose projected Mexican masterpiece got completely out of control and was never properly finished. The Spaniard, Luís Buñuel, on the other hand, whose *Los Olvidados* (*The Beggars*) is probably taken as being more typical of Mexican life as the world would like to imagine it than any other film could possibly be, left a deep legacy of black comedy and satirical social commentary.

In the late 1930s the Mexican cinema had already developed a crop of distinguished stars—Pedro Armendáriz, Dolores del Río, and the uniquely Mexican comedian 'Cantinflas' (Mario Moreno). After the war, as in the United States, the stars came to dominate the scene. Commercial considerations were primary, and many critics lamented the disappearance as they saw it of the bold experimentation of the early days. Professionalism is the keynote of the modern Mexican cinema industry, a major export industry undertaking everything from full-length features, through musicals, cartoons and 'shorts', to advertising commercials. Nevertheless, it is very much alive, and has played a major role in the education and entertainment of the Mexican people in their years of growth and expansion.

RADIO AND TELEVISION

The Mexicans were very quick to recognise the potentialities of the new medium of radio. While most other countries were still thinking of it in terms of vast military or emergency communications, the Mexicans were already experimenting with broadcasting as early as 1918. When, under President Obregón, radio was brought under the control of the central government and given some form of organisation, the model followed was that, not of Europe, but of the United States. Commercial broadcasting was introduced in 1923. Today, broadcasting is governed by the law of 1960 which set up a national council of radio and television with powers to regulate both services. There were in 1971 636 broadcasting and 64 television stations. These are organised in four networks, of which the largest is Radioprogramas de México. In addition to the capital, this network controls transmitters in, among other places, Monterrey,

Guadalajara, Oaxaca, Sabinas, Coahuila, Chihuahua, La Piedad, Nogales, Mérida and Tijuana.

The number of radio receivers in Mexico in 1971 was over 14 million. This figure represents roughly one for every four in the population, but in practice many of these sets are in public places where their transmissions can be heard by a great number of people. This is even more true of the 2,980,000 television sets, the numbers of which are growing very rapidly under the forced competition between the numerous local manufacturers or assemblers of radio and television receivers. The market for these is far from saturated. As for the actual programmes, inevitably these suffer from the commercialisation implicit in advertising, and the announcers speak in a vigorous enthusiastic accent in which there is more than an element of North American.

MUSIC

The love of music in Mexico goes back to pre-Columbian times. The influence of the Spanish idiom, however, is very great, and the characteristic vigour and tempo of Spanish music are supplemented by the interest in indigenous musical instruments. The guitar still forms the indispensable accompaniment to all Mexican music, but the gourd has gained international status as an instrument in its own right, as has the wooden rasp. Mexican folk singers, particularly in the south of the country, rely heavily on the wooden xylophone (*marimba*) played simultaneously by several people. Music forms an integral part of all fiestas and public occasions.

Two other alien influences on Mexican music have been of great importance. First of all, there was the influence of the French, who gave rise to the familiar *mariachis*. The *mariachis* consists of a small band primarily made up of guitars and violins which plays in the streets and parks and in restaurants. Their music forms a basic part of the diet of the Mexican radio listener. A later importation, this time from the United States, is the brass band. Mexicans delight in its virile sonorous sound, and the end of the nineteenth century and the beginning of the twentieth saw the sprouting, in the plaza of nearly every Mexican town of any size, of an elaborate and attractive-looking wrought-iron bandstand. Many of these are still in use. Perhaps this diverse musical heritage has in a way been confusing, for certainly Mexican composers have not, on the whole, attained the world-wide renown of, say, the Brazilians.

However, in one respect at least they have achieved something quite uniquely Mexican. This is the Ballet Folclorico, centred upon the Palace of Fine Arts in Mexico City. The palace itself is quite remarkably ugly, a white marble building in the Second Empire style completed as a monument to independence and to the glory of General Díaz. Today, almost entirely as a result of the enterprise of one woman, Amalia Hernández, who brought together the arts of dancing and music, already innate in Mexican culture, and used her own financial resources to give it a start, it is a 'must' for all visitors.

THE VISUAL ARTS

The visual art in which modern Mexicans have excelled beyond all comparison is mural painting. Mural painting is so much part of architecture that it is often forgotten how much Mexicans have interested themselves in the latter art also, and to what an extent their country has been one of the centres of inspiration of the modern movement in architecture. José Villagran García was the first man to bring the new style to Mexico with his Granja Sanitaria at Tacuba in the Federal District. The Modernist school which he created not only had the advantage of revolutionary simplicity, stressing practicality and comfort, but also had the functional purpose of creating buildings of substantial size that were resistant to earthquake shock. In the 1950s and 1960s the enthusiasm for large expanses of curtain walling in glass—not an unmixed blessing in the climate of Mexico—has considerably eroded this distinctive contribution, with what results is not yet absolutely certain. Thus the Latin American tower in Mexico City, by Leonardo Zeevaert, which is the highest building in Mexico and one of the highest in the Western hemisphere, is a rather standardised skyscraper which might be found almost anywhere; only in foundations, not visible to the public, does the element of earthquake protection remain as an essential part of the whole structure. More practical are the triangular structures that house the national railways and the celebrated pyramidal Edificio Símbolo which stands in the centre of the Workers' Housing Project near the Plaza de Tres Culturas.

Mexico has learnt from the pre-Columbian archaeological discoveries, and has passed through the period of stiff and over-slavish copying of pre-Columbian forms; her Spanish heritage, undoubted though it is in her domestic architecture, is currently somewhat in eclipse. The field of mural painting is purely Mexican, since the Mayas decorated the insides of their buildings with paintings, and the craftsmen who did this work were the same as those employed by the Spaniards on the decoration of the interiors of their churches, where their work may still be seen. Although influenced by external forms, there is a degree of continuity in mural painting which owes its revival to the Revolution itself. The muralists of the Revolution sought to propagate its values in the most immediate and direct way possible by conveying to the largest number of people the things for which it stood in a single location in a significant public building. The most celebrated of the artists of the mural school must be Diego Rivera (1886–1957). Regarded by the Mexicans themselves as one of the great artists of the century, his work is most familiar to visitors to Mexico through his great series of frescoes on the main staircase and balcony of the National Palace, in which he interprets in the spirit of socialist realism the development of the history of Mexico from pre-Columbian times to the present. Before this, however, lay more than a decade of development of mural painting since its revival by him in 1922 in the Bolívar Amphitheatre in the University of Mexico. It was Vasconcelos who, as secretary of education, gave him the opportunity to decorate the halls of the ministry in the 1920s and was responsible for the resurgence of the art. Like Rivera, David Siqueiros (d 1974) showed in his work his Marxist convictions. When commissioned to paint murals in the Rockefeller Centre in New York, Siqueiros was discovered to have embellished them with a large central portrait of Lenin. The painting itself was completely destroyed, but the work was redone in a Mexican setting and can still be seen today. Unfortunately for Siqueiros, he outlived the popularity of the Marxist message in his native country and was even imprisoned for a time by the government which shortly afterwards regretted its action and summoned him back to his last commission, the painting of a substantial mural work in the Palace of Chapultepec itself. The third of the three greatest Mexican mural painters, José Clemente Orozco (1883–1949), was more of a visionary; his greatest works, now in Mexico, are his murals in the Palace of Fine Arts (1934), but there are many others in the United States.

Orozco and Siqueiros both painted also on canvas, the latter not entirely from choice during his later years. There are, however, many other painters in oils in Mexico, and the art is generally in a flourishing state. Outside the capital, the most famous art centre is the colonial town of San Miguel Allende.

LITERATURE AND THE PRESS

Mexico, which can boast of the first true novel published in Latin America, already enjoyed a considerable literary activity in the colonial period. Today it is the greatest centre of activity of publication in the Spanish-speaking world; only Spain itself and Buenos Aires have anything to compare with it. One of the reasons for this is historical, namely the fact of the Revolution and the existence of the important school of novelists beginning with Martín Luis Guzmán in 1916, who have commemorated the Revolution itself. The other is political; for long periods of time in the present century publication in both Spain and Argentina has been considerably restricted, while publication in Mexico, particularly for left-wing and radical views, is relatively free. In 1971 titles published numbered 4,439, of which 1,921 were classified as being in the natural sciences and 1,124 in social science.

Mexicans are enthusiastic newspaper readers. In 1970 there were 208 daily newspapers with an aggregate circulation of nearly 5 million. About half of these circulated in the capital, or roughly one newspaper for every four in the greater metropolitan area, so over the country districts the average circulation must be as low as 25 for every 1,000 population. On the other hand, given the average size of the Mexican household, the figure for the capital must represent near saturation, and for the country at large a very significant medium of communication.

Mexicans also have access to 873 public libraries holding a total 3,149,000 volumes. For the scholar, moreover, Mexico is a major centre of research for Latin America, with the resources of two national libraries totalling 870,000 volumes and 256 university libraries with combined holdings of over a million and a half volumes.

9
Hints for Visitors

CLOTHING

Because the climate in Mexico depends on height, not latitude, you can visit it at any time of year. The rainy season is between May and October; that is to say, during that time, there are likely to be one or two heavy showers a day, usually in the afternoon or evening, but otherwise the sun shines and it can be exceedingly hot by day. The main tourist season tends to be between November and March, when it is winter in the United States, and just after the rains the landscape tends to look at its best.

The diversity of climate presents few problems to the male traveller who takes a lightweight suit, a couple of pairs of lightweight trousers, and as many drip-dry shirts as he feels a need for. Women, of course, with modern non-crease fabrics, have no problem. Mexicans are (except at holiday resorts, where beachwear is accepted all day long) rather formal. They will inevitably wear suits for business, and a dark suit or jacket and tie will be wholly acceptable for dining in restaurants. The sensible traveller will do as they do; similarly when at a resort town he will wear casual slacks and sandals, elegant and expensive if his purse will run to it.

Viewing antiquities can be strenuous and there is usually not much cover from the sun. In the lowlands of Yucatán it is a good idea to avoid the middle of the day for travelling or sightseeing, and a long-sleeved shirt or blouse to protect against sun by day and occasional mosquitoes by night is a good idea, too. Women should wear comfortable flat-heeled shoes.

During the rainy season visitors are usually advised to bring an umbrella and raincoat. Of the two a lightweight raincoat is much the less inconvenient to carry, and can be used as an extra layer of clothing when it gets cool in the evening at Mexico's high altitudes. Neither, however, offers any real protection against the torrential, but fortunately extremely brief, downpours which the Mexicans term 'showers', and the only sensible thing to do if the clouds loom up is to take cover within the next thirty seconds. Fortunately, too, you can see the clouds begin to build up over the mountains in most places before they turn black and threatening, and plan your route accordingly.

TRAVEL DOCUMENTS

Visitors to Mexico, other than for visits of not more than seventy-two hours to towns near the United States border, require a tourist card if they are over the age of fifteen. Children under fifteen can be included on a parent's card. If travelling alone in Mexico, minors must carry in addition to their card a valid passport or birth certificate and a notarised letter in duplicate, signed by both parents, authorising them to make the journey. Tourist cards are issued by all Mexican consulates and tourist offices, by airlines flying into Mexico and at the frontier. US and Canadian citizens must present proof of citizenship; citizens of the United Kingdom and colonies a valid passport. Cards can be valid either for a single entry or for multiple entries, but in either case are valid only for six months and may only be renewed within Mexico if the bearer can produce a doctor's certificate that he is unfit to travel. No charge is made for the issue of tourist cards. If applying by post, remember to enclose a stamped self-addressed envelope for the return of your tourist card together with your passport or other proof of citizenship.

Special arrangements apply to persons wishing to do business or study in Mexico, and they should enquire for details at the nearest Mexican consulate, which can also advise on regulations governing fishing or hunting. Tourists bringing pets into Mexico must have two certificates, both certified by a Mexican consul (fee payable). One certificate must be from a veterinary surgeon certifying that the pet is in good health, and the other that it has been vaccinated against rabies within the previous six months. It is wiser to arrange to leave your pet at home.

HOW TO GET THERE

The obvious way to arrive in Mexico is by air. Less obvious but much cheaper, if that is a consideration, and certainly much more interesting, is to travel by bus from the United States. Visitors from the United Kingdom can take advantage of the new cheap transatlantic fares, and also of the direct services now available to Miami and New Orleans. Visitors from the United States can of course travel by car. Hertz and Avis both operate within Mexico, as do a number of Mexican car-hire firms, but although they do hire out smaller cars than are usually available in the United States (the Volkswagen 'beetle' is the most common), their rates are not particularly low. Visitors from the UK arriving in Mexico City directly from their home country would probably be well advised to get used to the traffic for a few days before attempting to drive in the capital itself. They will, however, provided they remember to drive on the right, find no difficulty on the open roads.

Travellers by car from the United States are advised to have their cars properly serviced before leaving, carry adequate spares and (especially if travelling with children) a good supply of drinking water, and to remember that distances between filling stations, which are only usually encountered in towns, are much greater than they have been accustomed to. The combination of heat and altitude can overheat a radiator surprisingly quickly, so keep an eye on the temperature gauge.

Mexico's first-class buses are speedy and air-conditioned. The rest stops are about as frequent and of about the same standard as are generally found in the United States in the south and west, and the economy-conscious traveller will buy food and carry cool drinks to consume on the way. Remember if going into the United States that the Americans have an obsession with keeping agricultural products (eg apples and oranges) out of their country, and if you fail to eat them before you reach the border they will be politely taken away and destroyed. The same goes for the straw in which small, fragile and no doubt expensive pottery or glass souvenirs may have been packed.

Seats are reserved on all first-class buses. If you plan to break your journey (you are allowed two stopovers), remember to book the next leg of your journey before you leave to go to your hotel. In Mexico City there is a central bus-ticket agency serving six major bus lines which will answer your questions and make reservations. You can even order tickets by telephone to be delivered to your hotel. Incidentally, the city buses in the capital are extremely cheap and a very interesting way to travel. But many Mexicans themselves use taxis, either of the *pesero* variety or the more usual sort with meters which you use for one journey only.

HOTELS

Hotels, motels and furnished apartments are classified by the Tourist Department, which fixes the rates and requires them to be prominently displayed in each room. Overcharges should be reported to the department. Categories range from AA (de luxe), through A (first class), B (standard), C and D to E. Variety is surprising and within the categories themselves the décor may range from full Spanish colonial to plastic counters and ultra-modern. Indeed, many combine both. Not all smaller hotels have restaurants attached, and in major cities most hotels offer the so-called European plan (without meals). American plan (full board, often modified to drop the midday meal) is normal at resort hotels. Prices are low by United States standards; not so low by the standards of Britain or Europe, but there are many admirable guest houses (*pensiones* or *casas de huespedes*) where the accommodation is simple but adequate, the prices low and the atmosphere much more interesting. Virtually everyone in hotels and waiters in restaurants have to be tipped—the standard rate is about 15 per cent provided that you do not tip less than a peso. Porters and bellboys expect a minimum of 5 pesos or a peso per bag handled, and chambermaids 2 pesos a day. Ten per cent of the bill is the rule in beauty parlours and barber shops.

Hotel staff can advise on or arrange excursions to all the principal tourist attractions through the services of the tourist companies, which are numerous and very well organised. Excursions may, depending on the size of the party, be by bus, by car or by limousine, and guides speak excellent English in the American idiom, with which it is as well to become acquainted. The diligent and the more than merely curious can see most of what they want to see with the aid of guidebooks. It would be a sensible idea to take along a good electric torch for exploring the dark interiors of some of the more interesting monuments. Guides have, if anything, either a small book of matches or a torch which is on the point of expiring, although some of the more popular attractions are now illuminated inside. Photographers should not forget a flashgun, if they have one, as shadow contrasts are in any case very great. Guides expect tips, and on allday excursions the rate is 10 pesos per day per person, in addition, of course, to the charge for the excursion. Guides are licensed and must show credentials on request.

FOOD AND HEALTH

Food is a matter for diligent experiment. In general the best value can be expected where the Mexicans themselves eat, and it is comforting to remember that an unprepossessing exterior is no guide to the cleanliness or the quality of the food inside. Particularly at the altitudes of the central plateau it is advisable to eat the main meal, as the Mexicans do, about 2 pm and not to hurry it. A light meal may be eaten at the usual hour of 9 pm, but in any case it is advisable not to eat a heavy meal late at night. However, this is largely a matter of comfort. If you are going to eat unfamiliar food —and what is the point of doing anything else?—then you may very well not avoid a stomach upset, and no amount of cleaning your teeth with bottled water, taking stomach-settling tablets or adjusting your eating hours is likely to prevent that. If you do have a stomach upset, go to the nearest chemist (*pharmacia*) and ask them to sell you a suitable preparation, which is available without prescription and is the only effective remedy. If you should happen to be taken more seriously ill when in Mexico City, get a taxi and ask to be taken to the 'Hospital Inglés'. This is the popular designation of the American-British Cowdray Hospital, whose charming staff are most efficient and all speak English. Charges are surprisingly low, but insurance is a wise precaution anyway.

LANGUAGE

Generally speaking it is, of course, a good idea to have some basic idea of the language of the country, the better to enjoy it. Mexican Spanish resembles closely that of the Peninsula but lacks the intrusive lisp which became fashionable there only in the eighteenth century. This absence may present some problem to English visitors who have already learnt the language in England. All visitors, however, should make the effort to learn at least the Spanish for 'please' and 'thank you', since their omission automatically creates something of a climate of offence. Many Mexicans speak English so well that it is positively embarrassing, and most people who have anything to do with the tourist circuit know some English. It is also valuable to be able to read shop signs.

TOURIST INFORMATION

Motorists should ensure that all their papers are in order before entering the country, which means a car-registration certificate for an owner driver, together with a notarised certificate from the owner in other cases giving permission to drive in Mexico, and Mexican car insurance, which can be obtained either from agents in the United States or at the frontier. Trailers must be insured, too.

Spares that motorists should carry include, apart from the spare wheel, jack etc, fan belt, inner tube, fuses, petrol can, tyre-pressure gauge, footpump, screwdriver, pliers and adjustable wrench. An alarm or other anti-theft device will increase peace of mind. The weakest point of the car is the driver, who is going to get hot, tired and uncomfortable. He will find it useful to take a steering-wheel cover, something to protect him from his driving seat (which can get very hot), paper tissues, toilet paper (seldom available on the road), washing gear and towel.

Mexican road signs are international in form with the legends in Spanish. These should be carefully memorised. The only one that requires unusual treatment is the sign for a narrow bridge, *puente angosto*, for there are a great many of them and the rule of the road is that the first driver to flash his lights when approaching one has right of way. So do *not* take it as an invitation to go first!

INFORMATION

Camping is legal in Mexico and there are a number of caravan sites (trailer parks). Further details about this and all other tourist information can be obtained from the nearest office of the Mexican National Tourist Council, who in addition to being responsible for the highway patrols on Mexico's main roads, maintain an excellent information office in Mexico City at Reforma 45 (telephone 35-81-20). Information on current events in the capital is available free in English-language broadsheets.

SOUVENIRS

Souvenirs available depend on your resources. All local products are available in Mexico City—at a price—but it is much more fun to look for them in their proper place of manufacture, where it is customary in most cases to bargain over the price. When approaching large articles with the enthusiasm they deserve, such as the *sarapes* (blankets) of Oaxaca and Tlaxcala, the pottery of Tlaquepaque and Tonalá, near Guadalajara, the silk shawls (*rebozos*) of San Luis Potosí, or the wrought iron of Puebla, the home of blue tiles (*azulejos*), it will be wise to try to envisage how they will actually look in your own home. Unless you are very fortunate, or have the money to undertake a complete Mexican room, they are all too likely to stick out like a sore thumb. As the Spaniards themselves learnt, one of the best souvenirs of Mexico (if you can afford it) is the silver of the mines near Taxco. Make sure it has the Mexican mark of origin and keep the receipt in the unlikely event that the customs officer asks to see it on leaving the country. You will have some more explaining to do when you get to your own customs, too, but it is worth it.

Index

Acapulco, 44, 116, 127
Adobe (mud brick), 82–3
Advertising, 94, 150–1
Agrarian reform, 49, 55, 99–100, 107
Agriculture, 17, 18–20, 45, 46, 97, 99–101, 102, 135
Aguascalientes, 30, 41, 67
Air Force, 77–9, 126
Air travel, 79, 116, 124–6, 158
Alemán, Miguel, 113, 138
Alfaro, José María, 78
Archaeological sites, 20, 23, 46, 116, 147–8, 156–7
Architecture, 20, 37, 40, 82–8, 115, 138–9, 152–4
Army, 61–2, 76–7, 136
Art, visual, 20, 139, 152–4
Artists, 134, 139
Aztecs, 11–12, 14, 21, 23–4, 36, 39, 41, 80, 106, 108, 111, 119, 143–4

Baja California
  peninsula, 12, 16, 47–8
  Norte, 30, 47–8, 74
  Sur, 30, 48, 68, 97
Bajío, the, 42
Balance of payments, 76, 100, 110, 116
Ballet, 152
Bananas, 49, 101
Beans, 19, 90–1, 99–101
Belize, 11, 46, 53
Braceros, 13, 50
Braniff, Alberto, 78
Brazil, 107, 152
Budget, Federal, 58, 132

Bullfighting, 146
Bus services, 41, 68, 93, 123–4, 139, 159

Cabinet, 59–60
Cabrera, Luis, 55
Cactus, 16, 18, 80, 92, 142
Cafés, 142
California, 13, 31, 48
Calles, Plutarco Eliás, 35, 61
Campeche, 30, 45
Camping, 162
Capital, 71–2, 75–6
Cárdenas, Lázaro, 28, 59, 61, 65, 99, 112–13, 115, 137
Carranza, Venustiano, 49, 55–7, 81
Cars, 72, 93, 124, 128 ff, 158 ff
Cattle, 102, 105
Cement, 72, 75, 83, 111, 115
Census (1970), 30, 88
Central America, 12–13, 17, 45, 60
Cerro de Mercado, 108
Chapultepec, 40–1, 140, 143, 147, 154
Chemicals, 75, 110–11, 113
Chiapas, 30, 35, 45
Chicanos, 13, 53
Chichén Itzá, 32, 147–8
Chicle, 101, 106
Chihuahua, 151
Chillies, 19, 90–1, 99–101
Chilpancingo, 30, 44
Chocolate, 91, 101
Cinema, 102, 140, 148–50
Ciudad Juárez, 121
Civil Service, 62, 69
Climate, 14, 16–18, 20, 38, 42, 45–8, 156

164

Index

Clothing, 92–3, 156–7
Coahuila, state of, 30, 108
Coal, 107–8
Coatzacoalcos, 127
Coffee, 45, 91, 100–1
Colima, 30, 43
Commerce, 117–18
Congress, 26, 58, 63–5
Constitution: (1813), 44; (1824), 26, 55; (1857), 54–5, 60, 65; (1917), 28, 54–8, 65
Consumer goods, 82, 93–4, 108
Copper, 46, 47, 109–11
Core, 19, 21, 24, 41–3, 88, 116
Corn *see* Maize
Corruption, 69
Cortés, Hernán, 12, 14, 23, 95, 132, 146
Costa Rica, 13, 119
Cotton, 100, 116
Courts, 65–7
Cowboys, 46, 102
Crafts, 163
Crops, 99–101
Cuauhtémoc, 24
Cuba, 60
Cuernavaca, 30, 44, 127, 129
Currency, 69–70

Death, causes of, 96
Díaz, Porfirio, 27–8, 32, 40, 44, 49, 79, 109, 114–15, 132–4, 149
Diseases, 21, 95–6
Domestic help, 94
Donkeys, 102, 105, 119
Drinks,
  alcoholic, 18, 72, 73, 92, 108, 142
  soft, 72, 92
Driving licences, 130
Durango, 30, 43, 108

Eagle, Mexican, 80
Echeverría, Alvárez Luis, 69
Economy, 16, 28, 57, 75–6, 109, 115
Education, 90, 132–41
  further, 140
  primary, 132, 133, 134, 135–6
  secondary, 133, 134, 136–7
  technical, 133, 137–8
  university, 95, 133, 134, 138–40

Ejidos, 97, 100
Electoral system, 57, 63, 64–5
Electric power, 16, 43, 68, 72, 89, 92, 114–15
Entertainment, 73, 117
Europe, 11, 82, 116, 118, 126, 150
Exports, 70, 100–1, 127

Family, 36, 67, 87, 97
Federal District, 30–1, 39–41, 42, 66, 68, 79, 97, 141, 152
Federal system, 11, 54, 56
Fiestas, 143
Fishing, 53, 97, 106
Food, 18–19, 72, 75, 99–101, 161
Foreign investment, 75–6
Foreign policy, 59–60
Forestry, 72, 97, 99, 105–6
France, 27, 40, 49, 78, 88, 99, 120, 145, 151
Frontera, 127
Frontiers, 11, 12, 16, 24, 120–1, 129

Gas, 47, 113–14
Geology, 14, 16, 22, 38
Germany, 64, 77, 124
Goats, 102, 105
Gobernación (interior), secretary of, 59, 80
Gold, 76, 108–11
Golondrinas, 108
González Bocanegra, Francisco, 81
Green Angels, 130
Guadalajara, 30, 31, 43–4, 122, 151
Guadelupe Hidalgo, 25
Guatemala, 11, 45, 46, 53, 121, 129
Guaymas, 127
Guerrero, state of, 30, 43, 44, 108, 141
Guerrero, Vicente, 23, 44
Guerrillas, 43, 53, 57
Gulf of Mexico, 12, 13, 41, 45, 47, 48–9
Guzmán, Martín Luis, 155

Health, 94–6, 161
Hermosillo, 30, 63
Hidalgo, Fr Miguel, 25, 145
Hidalgo, state of, 20, 30
Historical landmarks, 22–9

Horses, 102, 105, 119
Hospitals, 95–6, 161
Hotels, 40, 88, 116–17, 159–60
Housing, 36, 81–90, 92
Huerta, Victoriano, 149
Hurricanes, 47

Iguanas, 129
Imports, 70, 100
Income Tax, 70–2
Independence, 13, 25–6, 42, 80, 145–6
Indians, 20, 22, 24, 44, 45, 49, 132, 141, 144
Industry, 37, 43, 76, 97, 115
Iron, 46, 47, 107–8
Irrigation, 16, 47, 48
Iturbide, Agustín de, 25, 26, 80

Jade, 108, 119
Jalapa, 30, 78
Jalisco, 30, 43, 139
Juárez, Benito, 27, 44, 146

Languages,
  English, 95, 162
  Indian, 11, 20–1, 36, 44, 95, 141
  Spanish, 21, 36, 95, 135, 148, 154–5, 161–2
La Paz, 48
La Piedad, 151
Legal System, 56, 65–7
Liberals, 25, 26, 27, 31–2
Libraries, 154
Life, expectation of, 96
Literacy, 102, 134, 135, 140–1
Literature, 154–5
Livestock, 102–5
López Mateos, Adolfo, 114, 122

Madero, Francisco I., 28, 41, 149
Mail, 130
Maize, 18–19, 82, 83, 90, 99–101
Maximilian, Emperor, 27, 41, 53, 120
Maya, 17, 20, 23, 36, 45–6, 77, 119, 147
Mazatlán, 35, 48, 79, 127
Medicine, 29, 94–5, 97
Medina, Bartolomé, 109
Mérida, 30, 46, 50, 63, 107, 127, 151

Mesilla Valley, 11, 26
Mestizos, 21
Mexicali, 48
Mexicanisation, 75–6
Mexico, city of, 24, 30, 31, 39–41, 42, 68, 79, 84, 87, 102, 105, 116–17, 120–1, 126, 127
Mexico, state of, 30, 39
Mexico, valley of, 12, 106, 120, 121
Michoacán, 30, 35, 67
Middle class, 28
Migration, 68, 88
Minatitlán, 127
Minerals, 16, 43, 56, 72, 122
Moctezuma I, 23
Moctezuma II, 23, 24
Monterrey, 47, 92, 107–8, 118, 124, 150
Morelos, state of, 30, 68, 121, 129, 143
Morelos y Pavón, José María, 68, 146
Motor vehicles, 72–3, 75, 93, 102, 123–4, 128–30, 158 ff
Mules, 105, 109, 119
Municipalities, 68, 73
Museums, 140
Music, 37, 140, 143, 151–2

Nacional Financiera, S.A., 74–5
Napoleon I, 25
Napoleon III, 27
National anthem, 81
National characteristics, 36–7
National coat of arms, 80
National flag, 80–1
Nationalisation, 113, 114, 122
National symbols, 80–1
National Workers Housing Fund, 73, 89–90
Navy, 77–8
Nayarit, 30, 43
Necaxa Falls, 114
Nogales, 122, 151
Northern plateau, 46
Nuclear energy, 115
Nuevo Laredo, 121
Nuevo León, state of, 30, 108
Nuno, Jaime, 81

Oaxaca, city of, 44, 121, 151
Oaxaca, state of, 30, 43, 67, 87, 116, 144, 147

Obregón, Álvaro, 56, 61, 134, 150
Obregón, Carlos Antonio, 78
Olmecs, 19-20, 22, 49
Olympic Games (1968), 29
Orozco, José Clemente, 154

Papaloapan Valley, 43
Parking, 129
Patzcuaro, Lake, 53, 106, 143
Pearson, Fred Stark, 114
Pearson, Weetman D., 112
Peasants, 28, 29, 61, 62
Petroleum, 47, 48, 75, 84, 111-14, 126, 127
Pigs, 102, 105
Police, 79-80, 129-30
Policemen, sleeping, 129
Political parties, 63-4
Pollution, 40, 128
Population, 28, 29-31, 65, 68, 88, 93, 95, 151
Portes Gil, Emilio, 61
Ports, 47, 48-9, 126-7
Poultry, 83, 90-1, 102, 105
Poza Rica, 84
President, 26, 40, 57, 58-60, 64, 65, 67, 77
Press, the, 154-5
Private consumption, 92-4
Progreso, 127
Public holidays, 143-6
Puebla, city of, 30, 44, 74, 88, 115, 123, 145-6
Pulque, 18, 92, 142

Querétaro, 27, 30, 42
Quintana Roo, 30, 68, 97

Radio, 82, 93, 140, 150-1
Railways, 11, 37, 120-3
Rainfall, 17-18, 42, 45-7, 157
Reform, the, 26, 32, 132
Refrigerators, 94
Regional development, 38, 74, 114
Religion, 22, 26, 31-6, 60, 80, 84, 87, 132, 135, 143-6
Restaurants, 117, 142
Revolution of 1910, the, 28, 32, 53, 57, 107, 112, 115, 123, 126, 153-4, 155
Rice, 91, 101

Río Bravo (Río Grande), 11, 14, 16, 50
Río Hondo, 12
Río Panuco, 48
Rivera, Diego, 153-4
Roads, 42, 119-20, 129-30, 162
Rodríguez, Abelardo, 74
Ruiz Cortines, Adolfo, 106, 122
Ruling party, 29, 57, 61-2

Sabinas, 108, 151
Saints, 84, 87, 143-6
San Cristóbal de las Casas, 50
Sanitation, 89
San Juan de Ulua, 78
San Miguel, Allende, 154
Santa Anna, Antonio López de, 26, 81
Sewing machine, 82, 93
Sheep, 102-5
Sierra, Madre, 42, 46-7, 109
Silver, 44, 76, 88, 108-11
Sinaloa, 30, 35, 43, 48
Siquieros, David, 154
Sisal, 46, 101, 107, 127
Social security, 72, 93-4, 96-8
Social services, 29, 31, 97
Socialism, 28, 32, 55, 60, 63, 154
Sonora, 30, 63, 127
Spanish colonial rule, 12-13, 24-5, 29, 42, 46, 77, 80, 95, 108-10, 115, 120, 132
Spanish Conquest, 12, 21-4, 49, 108
Spanish culture, 151-2
Spanish refugees, 22
Sport, 102, 139, 146-8
Squash, 19, 90, 100-1
States, 30, 38, 56, 64, 67-8, 73
Steel, 47, 75, 107-8
Stockraising, 46, 99, 102, 105
Suchiate, 11, 121
Sugar, 49, 72, 91, 100-1

Tabasco, 30, 45, 49, 127
Tacuba, 152
Tamaulipas, 30, 47, 48, 49, 52
Tampico, 47, 48, 112-14, 126-7
Tariffs, 94
Taxation, 56, 70-3, 74
Taxco, 44, 127

Taxis, 128, 159
Tehuantepec, Isthmus of, 19, 41, 47, 112–14, 121, 127
Telegraph, 130
Telephone, 72, 130
Television, 94, 150–1
Temperature, 17–18, 19, 42, 45, 47, 156
Tenochtitlan, 12, 23, 39, 80, 143
Texas, 11, 13, 26
Texcoco, Lake, 40, 143
Textiles, 75, 115–16
Theatre, 140
Tijuana, 151
Tipping, 160
Tobacco, 72, 108
Toltecs, 20–1, 144
Tomato, 91, 92, 101
Torreón, 47
Toscano, Salvador, 148–9
Tourism, 40, 116–17
Tourist information, 156–63
Traffic, 40, 123–4
Transport, 41, 117, 119–31
Travel documents, 157–8, 162
Tuxpam, 126
Tuxtla Gutiérrez, 30, 45

Unemployment, 98
United Kingdom, 63, 64, 77, 78, 112, 113, 121, 148
United States, 11, 13, 16, 26, 27, 35, 46, 47, 48, 49–53, 60, 63, 64, 74, 78, 79, 82, 88, 94, 95, 112–13, 115, 116, 118, 121–2, 123, 126, 127, 129, 148, 150, 152, 159

University of Mexico, 95, 133, 138–9, 140, 154
Urbanisation, 31

Vacations, 143
Vasconcelos, José, 133–4
Vegetation, 18–19, 45, 46
Vera Cruz, city of, 41, 48–9, 120, 126
Veracruz, state of, 30, 35, 43, 47, 48, 78, 84, 122
Villa, 'Pancho', 28, 55
Villagran, García, José, 152
Volcanoes, 41

Wages, 71, 73, 93
Water resources, 39, 42, 43, 74, 84, 89, 92, 109
Wines, 92
Wood products, 105–6
Workers, 28, 29, 56, 61, 62, 93, 96–7
World War I, 77, 112
World War II, 77, 113

Xochimilco, 143

Yucatán peninsula, 13, 16, 17, 45–6, 78, 116, 119
Yucatán, state of, 30, 45–6, 63, 107, 122, 127

Zapata, Emiliano, 28, 44, 55
Zeevaert, Leonardo, 153
Zihuatanejo, 108